SPHERES OF AUTHORITY

APOSTLES IN
TODAY'S CHURCH

Spheres of Authority

Apostles in Today's Church

C. Peter Wagner

WAGNER
PUBLICATIONS

Spheres of Authority
Copyright © 2002 by C. Peter Wagner
ISBN 1-58502-025-7
Library of Congress Control Number: 2002106746

Published by
Wagner Publications
11005 N. Highway 83
Colorado Springs, CO 80921
www.wagnerpublications.org

Cover design by
Jackson Knight Design
10 Boulder Crescent ,Suite 102
Colorado Springs, CO 80903
719-634-6727 www.jacksonknight.com

Interior design by Rebecca Sytsema

Rights for publishing this book in other languages are contracted by Gospel Literature International (GLINT). For further information, contact GLINT, P.O. Box 4060, Ontario, CA 91761-1003, USA. You may also send e-mail to glintint@aol.com, or visit their web site at www.glint.org.

2 3 4 5 6 7 8 9   08 07 06 05 04 03

TABLE OF CONTENTS

CHAPTER ONE

THE APOSTLES
HAVE SURFACED

We are now living in the midst of an epochal change in the structure of the church. I like to call it the "new apostolic age."

The Church in a New Phase

The church has entered a new phase ever since the third millennium began in the year 2000. Although others may see it differently, I am inclined to read church history as containing two genuinely apostolic ages. The first one lasted for about two hundred years; a couple of generations after the first of the New Testament apostles concluded their ministry. The second came into its own about 1800 years later, around the year 2001.

Having said that, I do not want to be misunderstood. I do not mean to imply that the church of Jesus Christ or the kingdom of God went into a suspension mode of some kind for 1800 years. It most certainly did not. Jesus said, "I will build my church" (see Mt. 16:18), and He has been doing so ever since. God's people on earth have been preaching the gospel, making disciples, and setting captives free non-stop. The true church has been with us down through the ages, sometimes larger, sometimes smaller, sometimes stronger, sometimes weaker.

Apostles Throughout History

I have no question that apostles have been present in the church throughout its history. However, forces have been quite obviously at work, both in the invisible world and in the visible world, to keep them as subdued as possible. But who could doubt, looking back, that Gregory Thaumaturgus or Martin of Tours or Patrick of Ireland or Benedict of Nursia or Boniface or Anselm of Canterbury or Savanarola or John Wycliff or Martin Luther or Francis Xavier or John Knox or John Wesley or William Booth or William Carey or Hudson Taylor were apostles? A biography of Dwight L. Moody by Wilbur Chapman, published back in 1900, carries the subtitle, "A Tribute to the Memory of the Greatest Apostle of the Age."[1]

Calling Moody "an apostle" in 1900, however, is an exception to the rule. Generally speaking, even those who unquestionably had the gift and ministry of apostle were not, with notable exceptions such as the Irvingites of the 1800s or the Apostolic Church of the 1900s, publicly recognized by the church as apostles per se. Historically apostles were kept, so to speak, beneath the surface after the first couple of centuries or so. But no longer. A growing number of Christian leaders are now recognizing, acknowledging, and affirming both the gift and the office of apostle. The apostles have surfaced!

It took us about 100 years to get to where we are now. The earliest precursor of this New Apostolic Age, at least to my knowledge, was the African Independent Church (AIC) movement which began around 1900. Over the century, growth of the independent churches far outstripped that of the more traditional mission churches across the African continent. More recently the Chinese house church movement developed along apostolic lines, producing what is arguably the greatest harvest of souls ever seen in one nation over a 25-year period. The strongest evangelistic force in Latin America in recent decades has been what some call the "grassroots churches," which operate on what we now recognize as apostolic principles.

The "New Apostolic Reformation"

My term for the new wineskin which God has provided for churches like these is the "New Apostolic Reformation." It is a "reformation" because we are currently witnessing the most radical change in the way of doing church since the Protestant Reformation. It is "apostolic" because the recognition of the gift and office of apostle is the most radical of a whole list of changes from the old wineskin. And it is "new" to distinguish it from several older traditional church groups which have actually incorporated the term "apostolic" into their official name.

If truly the Spirit has been speaking to the churches about the apostolic wineskin that I am describing in this book, it must be biblical. Actually, there are three Scripture verses which are the primary proof texts for recognizing the gift and office of apostle. Many other texts support this, but these three are core:

Ephesians 4:11
And He Himself gave some to be apostles,
some prophets, some evangelists,
and some pastors and teachers.

The "He" is Jesus, who gave gifts to His people when He ascended into heaven after rising from the dead and spending forty days with His disciples (see Eph. 4:8). He subsequently gave gifted *people* to the church on two levels: (1) the foundational or governmental level (4:11), and (2) the ministry level through the saints (4:12). The five foundational or governmental offices are apostle, prophet, evangelist, pastor, and teacher.

A common name for these five offices is "the ascension gifts," because Jesus first gave them at His ascension. Others frequently refer to them as "the fivefold ministry." This may not be the best term because "ministry" is mentioned, not in verse 11, but in verse 12 as the role of the saints, while apostles, prophets, evangelists, pastors and teachers are supposed to *equip* them to do their ministry. It is admittedly a minor point, but it is the reason why I mostly prefer "foundational or governmental offices."

Ephesians 2:20
[The household of God is] built on the foundation
of the apostles and prophets,
Jesus Christ Himself being the chief cornerstone.

A well-known hymn states that "The church's one foundation is Jesus Christ her Lord." This is true in a general, theological sense because there would be no church at all without the person and work of Jesus Christ. However, in the nuts and bolts of the growth and development of the church after He ascended and left the earth, Jesus apparently prefers to be thought of, not as the *foundation*, but as the *cornerstone*. The foundation of the church through the ages is to be made up of apostles and prophets. The cornerstone, in turn, is essential because the cornerstone holds the foundation together. But if a church has Jesus *without* apostles and prophets, it is probably not everything that God desires it to be.

The wording of this verse is another reason why I like to call apostles, prophets, evangelists, pastors, and teachers "foundational" offices.

1 Corinthians 12:28
And God has appointed these in the church:
first apostles, second prophets, third teachers,
after that miracles, then gifts of healings, helps,
administrations, varieties of tongues.

The numbers here, *proton* (first), *deúteron* (second), and *tríton* (third), indicate that this not simply a random selection of gifts and offices. *Proton* here should be interpreted to mean that apostles are first in order or sequence, with the

Apostles, working hand-in-hand with prophets, have the task of implementing what God wants done on earth in a certain season.

emphasis not necessarily relating to hierarchy. To put it simply, a church without apostles, other things being equal, will not function as well as a church with apostles.

It is interesting that the traditional church has understood apostles and prophets to be offices relegated to the past apostolic age, but not continuing in churches throughout history. Based on this assumption, teachers would then be first in order here in 1 Corinthians 12:28 by default. Since supposedly there are no longer apostles and prophets, teachers are next in line.

Much of Protestant denominationalism over almost 500 years has, in fact, been governed by teachers and administrators, not by apostles and prophets. What do I mean by that? When you think of it, most denominational executives are, in the final analysis, administrators. Most pastors of local churches, at least ever since the sermon became the central point of weekly congregational life, are assumed to be teachers, with the sermon being their primary vehicle for teaching.

It is rather fascinating that, over the centuries during which we have had church government backwards according to this Scripture, we have practically evangelized the world! Think of what will happen now that church government is getting in proper order! Administrators and teachers are essential for good church health, but administrators will be better administrators and teachers will be better teachers if the apostles and prophets are in place.

Post-World War II Apostles

Here in North America, God began to open doors for the reemergence of apostles right after World War II. Some churches and groupings of churches began to recognize the office of apostle back then. However, the movement eventually sputtered. As we look back to those days we hear terms such as "Latter Rain," "Restorational Movement," "Deliverance Evangelism," and "Shepherding Movement," just to name a few. The leaders of these movements had great expectations that what they had started would reform the whole church in their generation, but it did not happen. To all intents and purposes, these post-World War II movements of God no longer exist today, and those that do continue have relatively little influence.

However the leaders of these movements were true pioneers. Let's be clear—the post-World War II apostolic movements were initiated by God Himself. They were glorious. Huge numbers were saved, healed, delivered, discipled, sent out as missionaries, and personally revived. But many of the pioneers who led the movements made their share of mistakes. We shouldn't see that as strange.

Making mistakes goes with the territory of being a pioneer. Think of the pioneers who opened up the western part of the United States. They made their share of mistakes as well. They killed too many buffaloes. They broke promises they had made to the Indians. They ruined good farm land. But with all their mistakes, our pioneers laid the groundwork for what the United States is today and we take off our hats to them.

Let's also take off our hats to the Christian leaders of fifty years ago! They were the pioneers who began to shape the new wineskins for the body of Christ that we are blessed with today.

Intercessors, Prophets, and Apostles

While their efforts, post-World War II, may have sputtered, they did not die. God began speaking to the church once again about restoring the office of apostle in the early 1990s. This time the process was different. It was a bit more gradual, involving first of all the office of intercessor and then the office of prophet. The decade of the 1970s saw the beginnings of the emergence of the enormous global prayer movement that we see today. As a part of that, the body of Christ began to accept the gift and office of intercessor. In the 1970s and even the 1980s it was unusual, even odd, for churches to recognize certain members as "our intercessors." But no longer. The odd church today is the one which does not yet recognize intercessors.

During the 1980s the gift and office of prophet began to surface in churches. Not that prophets had been absent in previous years and centuries, but now their ministry was being understood by a much wider segment of the body of Christ. The prophets gained stature in the 1990s, and, although they have not arrived at perfection as yet, their ministry is broadly accepted and appreciated.

Looking back, I think that we can discern God's logic, so to speak, in bringing intercessors and prophets on the scene before apostles. The role of intercessors is essentially to stand in the gap and open the communication highways between heaven and earth. Once they are open and the voice of God can be heard more clearly, it is the role of the prophets to receive the divine messages directed to His people. Then apostles, working hand-in-hand with prophets, have the task of implementing what God wants done on earth in a certain season.

Parenthetically, there is at least some possibility that one of the handicaps of the post-World War II apostolic movement was that the way for the apostles had not been adequately opened for them by the intercessors and prophets.

A New Assignment in the 1990s

I am actually writing about these pioneering efforts through hearsay. While I have been in Christian ministry since 1955, the traditional evangelical circles that I moved in knew virtually nothing about the apostles and healing evangelists of those days. The brief references that I heard to them while I was in seminary in the early 1950s relegated them to the lunatic fringe. I really didn't tune in strongly to the apostolic movement until 1993 when I received a clear new assignment from God to raise apostolic ministry to the top of my personal agenda. That's not too long ago!

Which brings us to the matter of timing. Just think—the last half of the Twentieth Century which began post-World War II is less than 3 percent of all of Christian history! The time since the reemergence of this idea in the beginning of the 1990s is only one-half of one percent of the history of the church! The New Apostolic Reformation is very new, but it is strong. My sense is that this movement will not sputter!

Some Disagree!

However, there are some who disagree. Back in the pioneer post-World War II days, many highly respected Christian leaders took strong public positions against the fledgling apostolic movement. Whenever the apostolic leaders would make one of their higher profile mistakes—and many of them, in fact, did not finish well at all—the opponents were more than ready to say, "I told you so!" I strongly suspect that the major reason why the post-World War II movements did not carry the day as some expected they would was that the criticism, much of it being based on empirical facts, was simply too strong to resist.

Even today we find continuing criticism of the New Apostolic Reformation. Take, for example, Vinson Synan. Few would deny that Vinson Synan is today's Number One historian of the Pentecostal/charismatic movement. His book, *The Century of the Holy Spirit* (Thomas Nelson), is a landmark publication. My high esteem of Vinson Synan is precisely what leads me to choose him as a contemporary representative of what we could call the opposing view.

Here is what Vinson Synan writes: "It is axiomatic to say that anyone who claims to be an apostle probably is *not* one. An apostle is not self-appointed or elected by any ecclesiastical body, but is chosen by the Lord Himself."[2]

The U.S. Assemblies of God, again one of today's most highly respected Christian bodies, is even stronger in their opposition to the New Apostolic Reformation. During the post-World War II phase, their General Council in 1949 decreed that "The teaching that the Church is built on the foundation of present-day apostles and prophets" is "erroneous."[3] This was reiterated in their General Council of 2000. The denomination declared that the "teaching that present-day offices of apostles and prophets should govern church ministry" is a "departure from Scripture" and a "deviant teaching."[4]

Will This Movement Sputter?

I cite these criticisms, and I have many more in my files, to raise the question as to whether the current apostolic movement is in danger of sputtering like the last one did. I don't believe that it will, based on four observations:

1. We have learned from the mistakes of the pioneers, and we are determined not to repeat them.

2. This movement was preceded by the ministry of intercessors and prophets who are now part of its warp and woof.

3. The growing library of substantial books on different aspects of apostolic ministry that began appearing in the late 1990s is highly impressive. These authors are building a solid biblical, historical, and theological foundation for the movement.

4. Apostolic accountability has been heightened by the formation of many units of apostles who are holding themselves responsible to peers for their ministry and their character.

As I see the picture, God has given His church a new wineskin and He will be pouring out new wine into that wineskin for the foreseeable future.

Notes

[1] J. Wilbur Chapman, *The Life and Work of Dwight L. Moody: Presented to the Christian World as a Tribute to the Memory of the Greatest Apostle of the Age* (Chicago IL: J. S. Goodman & Co., 1900).

[2] Vinson Synan, "Who Are the Modern Apostles?" *Ministries Today*, March-April 1992, p. 47.

[3] 1949 Minutes of the General Council of the Assemblies of God, Resolution 7: "The New Order of the Latter Rain."

[4] "Endtime Revival—Spirit-Led and Spirit-Controlled: A Response Paper to Resolution 16," Adopted by General Presbytery, The General Council of the Assemblies of God, August 11, 2000, p. 2.

CHAPTER TWO

IS HE REALLY
AN APOSTLE?

You do not have to be around the apostolic movement very long before you hear someone say: "Is he really an apostle?" or "Is she really an apostle?"

Not only individuals who are observing the apostolic movement from outside ask this question. I have heard apostles themselves ask it about others. It is very legitimate to wonder how anyone can really know that someone else is a true apostle. In fact, if we can't end up giving a satisfactory answer to that question, the New Apostolic Reformation will find itself on shaky ground.

Let's look at it more closely. How come we don't hear, "Is he (or she) really a pastor?" Or "Is he (or she) really a teacher?" Or even "Is he (or she) really an evangelist?" After all, pastors and teachers and evangelists are as much a part of Ephesians 4:11 as apostles and prophets.

Comfort Zones

I think that the answer to that revolves around three things. First of all, it revolves around our comfort zones. Most believers today are more comfortable with teachers and pastors and evangelists than they are with apostles and prophets. Why is this the case? It is because apostles and prophets are so relatively new, as I pointed out in the last chapter.

Historically, there was probably never a time when there were no teachers in the churches of the world. Teachers have been with us since the first apostolic age. Pastors, however, came into their own only at the time of the Protestant Reformation when they replaced the unbiblical office of priest that had crept into the church. We have, therefore, been around pastors for five hundred years or so. Evangelists, much to the surprise of many, only began to be recognized in the days of Charles Finney around the mid 1800s. Still, the 150 years since then has been time enough to make us quite comfortable with the office of evangelist. Several denominational publications, for example, will regularly include a list of their official "evangelists" without anyone raising an eyebrow.

It is not surprising that, since the notion that God is actually raising up prophets and apostles in the church today is less than 20 years old, many are still uncomfortable when they hear about it. The good news is that more and more leaders have now started moving in the direction of affirming the validity of the offices of prophet and apostle. The apostolic comfort zone is definitely in a vigorous expansion mode these days.

Personal Wounding

The second reason why some may raise questions as to whether those who use the term "apostle" are legitimate goes back to personal wounding. In the last chapter I mentioned that our post-World War II pioneer apostles made some mistakes. A ripple effect of some of those mistakes was serious emotional damage to individuals and families who had been caught up in a structure that they found to be overly authoritarian, coercive, and manipulative. Their disillusion with some of the apostolic leaders of the time has, not surprisingly, carried over today. Fortunately, the wounds of many of them have been healed and they are moving on. Furthermore a new generation is now coming on the scene that does not tend to equate apostolic leadership with abuse as some of their parents may have done.

Apostolic Authority

The third reason why the question, "Is he (or she) an apostle?" is legitimate relates to the extraordinary authority resident in a bona fide apostle. Because it is so important, I want to explain this matter of authority in a bit of detail over the next page or so.

Apostles are as different from other members of the body of Christ as eyes or ears or lungs are from other members of the human body. What is it that makes them different? While there are several things that distinguish apostles from other members of the body of Christ, the major one that stands out over all the rest is their authority. This is reflected in 1 Corinthians 12:28: "And God has appointed these in the church: *first* apostles, second prophets, third teachers..."

In my book *Churchquake!*, which describes how churches operate in the New Apostolic Reformation as over against traditional denominations, I point out that by far the major difference is "the amount of spiritual authority delegated by the Holy Spirit to individuals."[1] The two operative words in that statement are "authority" and "individuals."

Where Is the Trust?

In traditional denominations the locus of authority is ordinarily found in groups, not individuals. That is why we are accustomed to hearing about deacon boards or sessions or boards of trustees or presbyteries or general councils or annual conventions or synods or general assemblies. In the New Apostolic Reformation, however, trust has shifted from groups to individuals. On the local church level, the pastor is now the *leader* of the church instead of an *employee* of the church. On the translocal level, the apostle is the one who has earned the trust of the pastors and other leaders, and trust inevitably imparts authority.

The apostle Paul had no inhibitions about asserting his apostolic authority. For example, back in his days there were some members of the church in Corinth who were asking, "Is Paul really an apostle?" He responded by informing them that not only did he have apostolic authority, but that he would even *boast* about it. "For even if I should boast somewhat more about our authority, which the Lord gave us for edification and not for your destruction, I shall not be ashamed" (2 Cor. 10:8).

Where does this extraordinary authority come from? I go into quite a bit of detail on this in some of my other books, but let me just summarize here the five major sources of apostolic authority:

1. *Apostles have a spiritual gift.* I elaborate on spiritual gifts in Chapter 4, so here I will simply affirm that there is such a thing as the spiritual gift of apostle. Knowing that they are apostles because God has chosen to give them the gift of apostle obviously provides apostles a solid foundation of authority.

2. *Apostles have an assignment or call.* All apostles have the gift of apostle, but not all have the same assignment. Again, this will be detailed in Chapter 4. Apostles who know their God-given ministry assignment know that they are in the will of God. That frees them to move in authority.

3. *Apostles have extraordinary character.* They have met the requirement that a church leader be "blameless" (see 1 Tim. 3:2). I'll say more about this in the next chapter, but meanwhile there is no doubt that holiness of character generates authority.

4. *Apostles have followers.* The chief external validation that an individual has the gift of apostle is that others recognize this and willingly submit to the apostle's authority.

5. *Apostles have vision.* Apostles receive revelation from God, and consequently they are able to say, "This is what the Spirit is saying to the churches right now." Making such a statement with credibility carries with it tremendous authority.

Self-Appointed Apostles

Vinson Synan, whom I quoted in the last chapter, is right when he says, "An apostle is not self-appointed or elected by any ecclesiastical body, but is chosen by the Lord Himself." In fact when you think of it, the term "self-appointed apostle" turns out to be a semantic oxymoron, since no valid apostle is self-appointed any more than valid pastors or teachers are self-appointed. True, there are false apostles and false pastors and false teachers who may in fact be self-appointed, but in this book I am addressing *true* apostles, not *false* apostles.

Having said this, God's decision to make an individual an apostle must be recognized and affirmed by real people. If someone says, "God has called me to be an apostle," but no one else agrees, I will have to doubt whether that person has accurately heard God. Question: "Is he (or she) really an apostle?" Answer: No!

For example, the Corinthians did not vote Paul in as an apostle. When he wrote them he clearly stated that his authority was given to him by the Lord Himself (see 2 Cor. 10:8). Now here is a strong statement: *To the degree that the Corinthian believers did not recognize that the Lord had made Paul an apostle, they were out of the will of God! That is a dangerous place to be!*

Gift vs. Office

This brings up the crucial difference between the gift and the office. They are not the same. The spiritual gift is given to a person through God's grace and by His choice. The Greek word for "grace" is *"charis"* which enters into the word for spiritual gift, *"charisma."* However, while we receive the gift by the *grace* of God, we receive the office through *works.* The office is not given to us by God, but by people. The office is a public recognition that an individual has a spiri-

---

An apostle is a Christian leader,
gifted, taught, commissioned,
and sent by God
with the authority to establish
the foundational government of the church
within an assigned sphere of ministry
by hearing what the Spirit
is saying to the churches
and by setting things in order accordingly
for the growth and maturity
of the church.

---

tual gift and that they are authorized to exercise that gift within the body of Christ. We must be aware that there are a number of people to whom God has given gifts, but who have not entered into their destiny because they have not yet earned their office.

The office of apostle is conferred by responsible people. When asking the question: "Is he (or she) an apostle?", one of the follow up questions needs to be: "Who else recognizes this person as an apostle?" Those who follow the apostle as subordinates have a significant role in this recognition, but even more important is the affirmation of apostolic peers. This is one of the reasons why apostles are now spontaneously gathering together in peer-level associations of one kind or another. For example, I lead the International Coalition of Apostles (ICA), designed to connect as many peer-level apostles with each other as possible. When this happens, there is a much broader mutual recognition of apostolic offices, thereby raising the credibility of contemporary apostolic ministry in general.

At times a given apostle will call upon apostolic peers who agree that he or she has the gift of apostle to set them into the apostolic office in a public ceremony. As a part of the maturing process of the apostolic movement, this is happening more and more frequently. In my opinion, just for the record, I think this act should be referred to as a "commissioning," not as "ordination." A reason for this is that, presumably, the apostle has previously gone through a public ceremony of *ordination* to the Christian ministry. Consequently, we are now *commissioning* an already-ordained minister.

Defining "Apostle"

A curious fact is that, in all of the recent literature that has been published on the gift and office of apostle, very few of the authors have offered a finely-tuned definition of what an apostle is. The most complete discussion of different approaches to a definition is found in David Cannistraci's

Apostles and the Emerging Apostolic Movement (Regal Books). Cannistraci's definition is: "An apostle [is] one who is called and sent by Christ to have the spiritual authority, character, gifts and abilities to successfully reach and establish people in Kingdom truth and order, especially through founding and overseeing local churches."[2] Harold Eberle is more concise: "A true apostle is a minister sent by God to accomplish a specific work."[3]

This is my fifth book relating to apostles. In none of the first four did I offer a definition of apostle. One of the reasons is that I was on such a rapid learning curve that I feared intuitively that any definition I came up with would probably soon have to be revised, perhaps many times over! Now, however, I am ready to take the risk and do my best to craft a definition that hopefully will not have to be revised too much down the road. Here is my suggestion:

An apostle is a Christian leader, gifted, taught,
commissioned, and sent by God with the authority to estab-
lish the foundational government of the church within an
assigned sphere of ministry
by hearing what the Spirit is saying to the churches
and by setting things in order accordingly for the growth
and maturity of the church.

I have attempted, as far as possible, to make this a bare-bones definition of apostle. My hope is that it clearly sets forth the non-negotiable, essential qualities of all apostles, regardless of what specific apostolic assignment God may have given to each one of them.

Apostles Are Different

It is very important to keep in mind that apostles are not all the same. Watchman Nee makes an interesting observation concerning three of the best known early apostles, Peter, Paul and John. He points out that the differences among the three do not make them opposed to one another, but complimentary. Nevertheless, they were different. Peter's primary task, for example, was to be a breakthrough person, one to cast a net into the sea, a pioneer, an evangelist. Paul, while he also did some of the above was essentially a builder, making known the mystery of Christ, bringing believers to the fullness of their destiny, setting churches in order. John came later when nominality and error were threatening the church. He was a restorer, bringing God's people back to a position they had lost.

Watchman Nee says, "We have Peter, concerned first with the ingathering of souls; we have Paul, the wise master builder; and then, when failure threatens, we have John introduced to reaffirm that there is an original purpose still in view, and one that, in the mind of God, has never been abandoned.... The practical point of what we have been saying is this, that it takes these three complimentary and interrelated ministries to make the Church perfect."[4]

It is precisely because apostles are different from one another that I am reluctant to expand the definition of apostle to include many common apostolic qualities that some true apostles might not share. To explain, I have made a list of sixteen apostolic characteristics that will be displayed by many, if not most, apostles, but, in my opinion, not by all. In doing this, I am aware that some will argue that certain of the items on my list should actually be included in the definition itself, meaning that if any individual would not score high on that certain point, they are not really an apostle. I greatly respect that point of view, and, who knows? They might be right!

However, my personal conclusion at the moment is that none of these characteristics should be considered a litmus test for answering the question of this chapter: "Is he (or she) really an apostle?" At the same time, all sixteen are biblical and they collectively enter into the total process of apostles "setting things in order," which is part and parcel of the basic definition of apostle.

- ◆ *Seeing Jesus personally.* Of course the original twelve saw Jesus, but so did Paul. "Am I not an apostle? Am I not free? Have I not seen Jesus Christ our Lord?" (1 Cor. 9:1). Paul did not see Jesus in the flesh, but Jesus appeared to him on the Damascus Road. According to an informal survey of the apostles whom I know today, about 20 percent have actually seen Jesus personally.

- ◆ *Performing supernatural manifestations such as signs and wonders.* "Truly the signs of an apostle were accomplished among you with all perseverance, in signs and wonders and mighty deeds" (2 Cor. 12:12). Almost every apostle I know has seen physical healing in their ministry, but not many have seen mass healings through the casting of their shadow as did Peter (see Acts 5:15). The application of this, therefore, might well be mostly a matter of degree.

- ◆ *Planting churches.* "According to the grace of God which was given to me, as a wise master builder I have laid the foundation and another builds on it" (1 Cor.

3:10). Planting churches is a very important apostolic characteristic that David Cannistraci includes in his definition which I quoted above.

♦ *Appointing and overseeing local church pastors (or "elders")*. Paul and Barnabas planted churches, then returned and "appointed elders in every church, and prayed with fasting" (Acts 14:23). Paul instructed Titus, a member of his apostolic team in Crete, to "set in order the things that are lacking, and appoint elders in every city" (Titus 1:5).

♦ *Settling disputes in the church.* The Corinthian believers were at each other's throats. Paul writes, "Now I plead with you, brethren, by the name of our Lord Jesus Christ, that you all speak the same thing, and that there be no divisions among you, that you be perfectly joined together in the same mind and the same judgment" (1 Cor. 1:10). Apostles are frequently called upon to do this.

♦ *Applying discipline including excommunication.* "It is actually reported that there is sexual immorality among you, and such sexual immorality as is not even named among the Gentiles—that a man has his father's wife!... In the name of our Lord Jesus Christ, when you are gathered together, along with my spirit, with the power of our Lord Jesus Christ, deliver such a one to Satan for the destruction of the flesh, that his spirit may be saved in the day of the Lord Jesus" (1 Cor. 5:1,4-5). Pastors are rarely equipped to take this kind of drastic action. Apostles, however, have few inhibitions about doing it when needed.

♦ *Leading the church in spiritual warfare.* Paul's word to the Ephesians is: "Put on the whole armor of God... for we do not wrestle against flesh and blood, but against principalities and powers" (Eph. 6:11-12). Few apostles are pacifistic. Although warfare may involve casualties, they are more than ready to lead the troops against the devil. As a guidebook, I recommend *End Time Warriors* by John Kelly (Renew).

♦ *Receiving revelation directly from God.* Paul also writes to the Ephesians: "By revelation He made known to me the mystery...which in other ages was not made known to the sons of men, as it has now been revealed by the Spirit to His holy apostles and prophets" (Eph. 3:3,5). Some apostles receive revelation directly, some through prophets, and some (probably most) both ways.

♦ *Providing spiritual covering for other leaders.* "I commend to you Phoebe our sister, who is a servant of the church in Cenchrea, that you may receive her in the Lord in a manner worthy of the saints, and assist her in whatever business she has need of you" (Rom. 16:1-2). "Now if Timothy comes, see that he may be with you without fear; for he does the work of the Lord, as I also do. Therefore, let no one despise him. But send him on his journey in peace" (1 Cor. 16:10-11).

♦ *Suffering physical persecution.* "For I consider that I am not at all inferior to the most eminent apostles...From the Jews five times I received forty stripes minus one. Three times I was beaten with rods; once I was stoned; three times I was shipwrecked; a night and a day I have been in the deep" (2 Cor. 11:8,24-25).

♦ *Imparting spiritual gifts.* Why did Paul want to visit Rome? Among other things, "For I long to see you, that I may impart to you some spiritual gift, so that you may be established" (Rom. 1:11).

♦ *Transgenerational impartation.* Another way of saying this is fathering or mothering children in the faith. "For though you might have ten thousand instructors in Christ, yet you do not have many fathers" (1 Cor. 4:15). An excellent resource for this point is *The Cry for Spiritual Fathers and Mothers* by Larry Kreider (House to House Publications).

♦ *Attracting and distributing financial resources.* "All who were possessors of lands or houses sold them, and brought the proceeds of the things that were sold, and laid them at the apostles' feet; and they distributed to each as anyone had need" (Acts 4:34-35). Most apostles have the financial resources necessary to implement the vision that God has given them.

♦ *Casting out demons.* "So that even handkerchiefs or aprons were brought from [Paul's] body to the sick, and the diseases left them and the evil spirits went out of them" (Acts 19:12). Not all apostles have deliverance ministries, but many do.

♦ *Breaking curses of witchcraft.* Paul broke the spirit of divination (witchcraft) in Philippi (see Acts 16:16-18), and directly confronted the occult sorcerer, Elymas in Cyprus (see Acts 13:8-11).

◆ *Frequent fasting.* As he displays his credentials as an apostle, Paul mentions "in fastings often" (2 Cor. 11:27).

Character is the *sine qua non*

As we read this list of what we expect from apostles, we realize that the requirements for this ministry are formidable. To whom much is given much is required. This chapter will go a long way to help us know how we should approach the question: "Is he (or she) really an apostle?" But none of these sixteen forms of ministry can substitute for a pure heart. The character of an apostle, which I explain in the next chapter, is a *sine qua non* for valid apostolic ministry.

Notes

[1] C. Peter Wagner, *Churchquake!* (Ventura CA: Regal Books, 1999), p. 75._

[2] David Cannistraci, *Apostles and the Emerging Apostolic Movement* (Ventura CA: Regal Books, 1996), p. 29.

[3] Harold R. Eberle, *The Complete Wineskin* (Yakima WA: Winepress Publishing, 1993), p. 26.

[4] Watchman Nee, *What Shall this Man Do?* (Fort Washington PA: Christian Literature Crusade, 1961), p. 18.

CHAPTER THREE

AN APOSTLE'S CHARACTER

It may be true that most, but not all, apostles plant churches and see Jesus and suffer physical persecution and minister in signs and wonders and do the rest of the things on the list in the last chapter. However, what would you think if I said: "Most, but not all, apostles exhibit exemplary character?"

This would, of course, set off alarm bells in your mind. Red lights would begin to flash! How could a person with notable character flaws expect others to follow their leadership? What peer-level apostles would affirm or commission someone who is living a life that does not meet God's standards of behavior?

Paul's Chief Sign

When I write about apostles, I quote First and Second Corinthians quite frequently. For example, when I made the list of 16 apostolic characteristics in the last chapter, I used Corinthians in nine of them. The main reason why those two New Testament books have so much information about apostles is because there was a group of believers in the church at Corinth who were aggressively denying that Paul was really an apostle. That did not sit well with Paul, as we could well imagine, and he strongly defended his apostleship in both letters.

One of the places where he does this is in 2 Corinthians 12:12 where Paul says, "Truly the signs of an apostle were accomplished among you with all perseverance, in signs and

---

*Apostles are apostles, not because
they are perfect, but partly because
they have met God's standards
of holiness and humility.*

---

wonders and mighty deeds." As we have already seen, signs and wonders are common among apostles. But in this particular statement, Paul lists a *character* trait—perseverance—before mentioning signs and wonders.

"Perseverance" is translated "patience" in the King James Version. This word has a deeper meaning than, for example, the proper attitude when you find yourself in a long, slow line in the supermarket. David Cannistraci says it means "remaining persistent in the face of opposition" and "Patience is staying anchored when everything around is getting off course."[1] When we look at a person with the purpose of evaluating whether or not they are a true apostle, character questions must come first. I repeat, character, above all other signs, is the *sine qua non* for apostolic ministry.

Bill Hamon agrees. He says, "The new breed of apostles will be motivated by the spirit of wisdom...They will minister in the faith that works by love...Their character will be in line with the fruit of the Holy Spirit...Their attitudes, actions, and relationships with others will be according to the attributes of agape–love as revealed in 1 Corinthians 13."[2]

I also like the way David Cannistraci puts it: "Signs, wonders and mighty deeds have their place to be sure, but having those graces and abilities in operation without the presence of character would be useless as well as harmful." He concludes: "Apostleship is a matter of character above any other single quality."[3]

Passing the Biblical Tests

The apostles whom I know well enough personally to form an evaluation of their character pass the biblical tests. This has not surprised me. In fact, it is exactly what I would expect. A person cannot be a true apostle without extraordinary character. This rather sweeping statement is based on an assumption. Since it is God, and God alone, who makes a person an apostle, my assumption is that God wouldn't trust the office of apostle to anyone who has not agreed to meet His standards of holiness and humility.

Please note that I have not used the word "perfection." It is my strong feeling that no individual here on earth is, or will ever be, perfect in the sense of having no room for improvement in attitudes, behavior, or relationships. The Greek word *teleios*, frequently translated "perfect," does not signify a flawless moral nature, but rather *maturity*. When Jesus says, "Therefore you shall be perfect [*teleios*], just as your Father in heaven is perfect" (Mt. 5:48), He means that we are to live up to everything that God wants us to be. I like the way *The Message* translates this verse: "Grow up. You're kingdom subjects. Now live like it. Live out your God-created destiny. Live generously and graciously toward others, the way God lives toward you."

Apostles Are High on the Scale

If we agree that no one can be perfect, let's also agree on something else. Let's agree that apostles are expected to be further up the scale toward perfection than other believers. Why do I say this? It is because God has a double standard of judgment. I know this will surprise some, but just consider what the Bible is saying in James 3:1: "My brethren, let not many of you become teachers, knowing that we shall receive a stricter judgment."

Another way of putting this is that God has one standard of judgment for leaders and another for the rest of the body of Christ. Teachers are used as an example of leaders in James. But 1 Corinthians 12:28 says: "And God has appointed these in the church: first apostles, second, prophets, third teachers." If teachers face a stricter judgment, it follows that apostles will be judged even more strictly.

Apostles are apostles, not because they are perfect, but partly because they have met God's standards of holiness and humility.

Apostolic Holiness

I believe that it is possible to live, one day at a time, without sin. Holiness is not some desirable, but elusive, ideal. Holiness is an attainable personal quality. The Bible says, "But as He who called you is holy, you also be holy in all your conduct" (1 Pet. 1:15). God would not require us to do something that was impossible for us to do, such as being holy in "all" (not "some" or "most") of our conduct.

When I say that we can live without sin, I do not believe that we can ever get to the place where it is not *possible* to sin. Yes, it is possible, even probable, that each one of us will sin, most likely more than once. However, when we do sin, we confess the sin and God forgives us and cleanses us. We must never let the sun set on an unconfessed sin. An occasional sin is not necessarily a character flaw. It becomes a character flaw, however, if we fail to deal with it immediately, and worse if we repeat the sin.

When Jesus' apostles, on two separate occasions one year and a half apart, asked Him to teach them to pray, Jesus gave them what we now know as the "Lord's Prayer." If we pray the Lord's Prayer daily, we will have what we need to keep on the track of holiness. When we pray, "Forgive my sins," it is good to review the last 24 hours to see if any sin might have gone unconfessed. If we are filled with the Holy Spirit, He will bring those sins to mind at that time, and we confess them. Then we pray, "Lead me not into temptation," believing that

God will answer that prayer. If He does, we will not sin because we will not be tempted all day long. To nail it down, we also pray, "Deliver me from the evil one," and if that prayer is answered as well, we will have protection throughout the day. When we go to bed, we can look back at a whole day of pleasing the Lord through our holy life.

I expect apostles to live holy lives because personal holiness is assumed in the detailed lists of qualifications for church leadership that we have in the Bible. Take, for example, 1 Timothy 3:1-7, in this case listing the requirements for a bishop, but requirements which, by extension, must apply equally, or even more, to an apostle. Few of the qualifications have to do with gifts or abilities such as leadership or casting vision or healings or prophecy or oratory or scholarship. Granted— teaching is there. But the bulk of the qualifications have to do with character: a solid family, self-control, maturity, hospitality, moderation, peacefulness, material contentment, and things like that.

Blameless with a Good Reputation

Actually, the most exacting requirements on the list are the first and the last: "blameless" and "having a good testimony among those who are outside." Apostles, in order to sustain their ministry as God has designed it, must be blameless. Paul is an example. How could he scold the Corinthian believers for all the moral failures and character defects on their part? It is because he himself was blameless. He was able to assure them: "For I know nothing against myself" (1 Cor. 4:4). This, in turn, allowed him to say with integrity: "Therefore, I urge you, imitate me" (1 Cor. 4:16).

Apostles who, for any reason, cannot say to their followers, "Imitate me," would do well to reevaluate the validity of their apostolic call.

Pride

One of the 1 Timothy 3 requirements for leadership is "not a novice, lest being puffed up with pride, he fall into the same condemnation as the devil" (1 Tim. 3:6). Pride is a sure fire blockage to apostolic ministry. And the temptation is always there because of the unusual amount of authority entrusted to apostles. One of the most frequent "canned" stereotypes that critics of the apostolic movement come up with is that apostles are arrogant, authoritarian, manipulative, self-promoting, and haughty—in a word, proud!

I personally have the privilege of knowing more apostles than the average person. Among the bona fide, God-anointed, powerful, productive, high-energy, task-oriented apostles whom I know—and those adjectives describe the great majority of them—I do not know one whom I could accuse of being proud. Superficially, I admit, some may outwardly seem to be proud in certain public settings, but rarely does that impression persist when you get to the heart level below the surface.

Apostolic Humility

Now, let me carry this one step further. When you think of it, no one could be a real, true, legitimate apostle who was not humble. What do I mean? I mean that we can take Jesus' axiom literally that: "Whoever exalts himself will be humbled, and whoever humbles himself will be exalted" (Mt. 23:12 NIV). Apostles hold one of the most exalted offices in the church, at least according to 1 Corinthians 12:28, "*first* apostles." The only way to become exalted, according to Jesus, is to humble yourself. Gordon Lindsay says, "True apostles will first manifest their apostolic ministry by humility."[4]

It would be good if we could lose some of our inhibitions against talking about humility. I know that it may be difficult to do, but I lost mine to the extent that I have written a whole book with the title *Humility* (Regal Books). In it, I actually advocate that we should begin talking about our own humility a bit more than we usually have in the past. Moses did. He wrote the words: "The man Moses was very humble, more than all the men who were on the face of the earth" (Numbers 12:3). Jesus did. He said, "I am humble and gentle" (Mt. 11:29 NLT). Paul did. He wrote, "I, Paul, myself am pleading with you by the meekness [i.e., humility] and gentleness of Christ" (2 Cor. 10:1). Paul even went so far as to equate his humility with Jesus' humility!

Let's keep in mind that humility is a choice. Jesus said that He would exalt those who *humble themselves.* Apostles who continue to see the blessing and anointing of God on their ministry have learned how to humble themselves. It takes time, but it gets easier with maturity. That's why, as we saw above, the Bible warns against putting novices in leadership positions, lest they be "puffed up with pride" (1 Tim. 3:6). If some apostles make the mistake of not humbling themselves, chances are that God will step in and humble them. If and when that happens it is too late. I am sorry to report that in the relatively short time that I have led the International Coalition of Apostles (ICA), I have had to dismiss four of them for serious moral failure. God humbled them. They were no longer "blameless." They may be restored somewhere down the road, but things will never again be the same.

Character is the *sine qua non* for qualifying and ministering as an apostle!

Notes

[1] David Cannistraci, *Apostles and the Emerging Apostolic Movement* (Ventura CA: Renew, 1996), p. 108.

[2] Bill Hamon, *Apostles, Prophets and the Coming Moves of God* (Santa Rosa Beach FL: Christian International, 1997), p. 39.

[3] Cannistraci, p. 107.

[4] Gordon Lindsay, *Apostles, Prophets and Governments* (Dallas TX: Christ for the Nations, Inc., 1988), p. 14.

CHAPTER FOUR

SPIRITUAL GIFTS AND APOSTOLIC ASSIGNMENTS

In Chapter 2, I suggested that a major source of apostolic authority would be the fact that God has given the spiritual gift of apostle to certain individuals of His choice. At that point I didn't elaborate, but I promised that I would expand on the issue of spiritual gifts later. Now I would like to spend some time on spiritual gifts because, surprisingly enough, I have discovered that the over all level of understanding of the biblical teaching on spiritual gifts, and the practical application of that teaching to present-day ministry, has not been particularly high among leaders of the New Apostolic Reformation.

Charismata and Charismatics

At first glance, this may seem strange because the large majority of apostles would see themselves as "charismatic," which means that they base a good part of their self-identity on the fact that they move in the *"charismata,"* the biblical word for "spiritual gifts." Consequently, spiritual gifts are highly important to virtually every apostle. Most of them frequently preach and teach on spiritual gifts. I suspect that it will surprise many of them to read in a book like this that it might be extremely advisable to attempt to lift our understanding of spiritual gifts to a new level.

So, let me explain.

George Barna's Wake-Up Call

Although I had felt for some time that the apostolic movement had a bit of room to improve in the area of spiritual gifts, I found myself keeping that issue on the back burner. My wake-up call, however, came from a sociological survey on spiritual gifts released by researcher George Barna in February 2001. Before I go on, I should explain that I have a higher than average personal interest in spiritual gifts. I have been teaching on the subject since 1950, and I have written two books on it. In fact *Your Spiritual Gifts Can Help Your Church Grow* (Regal Books) is the most popular of all my books, now in its 39th printing with over one-quarter million copies sold.

I say that to help us understand why I was so shocked at Barna's findings. I thought that the body of Christ was on a roll in understanding and ministering in spiritual gifts. I thought just about everybody was now catching on, and I must admit that I had secretly harbored some hopes that perhaps my book might have been helping. Wrong! One of George Barna's findings revealed that the number of born-again Christians who don't even believe that they have any spiritual gifts at all is actually increasing!

Here is what Barna discovered. In 1995 the percentage of born-again Christian adults who did not think they had any spiritual gift was 4%. Not bad. However by 2000 the percentage had risen from 4% to 21%! Think of what it means if this trend continues very long. It means that we could be on the threshold of a whole generation of impotent believers attending impotent churches! What a potential opening for attacks from the world of darkness! I think it is time to sound the alarm!

A secondary discovery that Barna made is that many Christians don't even know what the biblical spiritual gifts really are. Some include in their lists of spiritual gifts strange things like a sense of humor or poetry or a good personality or going to church, just to name a few.[1]

What does this have to do with apostolic ministry?

Seeking the Cause

It is one thing to know that our knowledge of spiritual gifts is taking a nose dive, but it is another thing to analyze this in order to understand what might be happening behind the scenes. Others, I admit, may come up with more insightful explanations, but meanwhile my own best shot associates this discouraging phenomenon, at least to some significant extent, to the apostolic movement.

The fastest growing group of churches in the U.S. during Barna's test period of 1995-2000 were churches of the New Apostolic Reformation. Granted, they are not the largest group. But their annual growth rate is the highest. While these churches are almost invariably evangelistically-minded, research shows that the bulk of their growth has come from transfers out of other churches, not from adult conversions. If it were true, then, that the members of these growing apostolic churches were receiving less than ideal teaching on the subject of spiritual gifts, that in itself could go a long way in explaining Barna's findings.

My hunch would be that if George Barna had asked his questions about spiritual gifts to two separate groups, namely traditional evangelicals as over against Pentecostals, charismatics, and new apostolic believers all taken together, the traditional evangelicals would have scored considerably higher. It is true that they may not speak in tongues or prophesy or heal the sick or cast out demons as much as the others, but they generally do have a clearer biblical understanding of how spiritual gifts are intended to operate in the whole body of Christ.

Keeping that in mind, many of the transfers of church membership in the U.S. in recent years have been from the more traditional evangelical churches to the apostolic churches, as Doris and I know from our personal experience. We did it in 1996. Granted, most of those who transfer membership will testify that their spiritual lives and relationship to the Lord have been kicked up a notch through their decision to change. I would not question that in the slightest. However, at the same time I would suspect that their understanding of how to use spiritual gifts in the church might well have slipped and thereby contributed to Barna's findings.

Why are many of the new apostolic churches weak on spiritual gifts?

Apostolic Spiritual Genealogy

It goes back to their spiritual genealogy. New apostolic churches for the most part (probably around 80%) are rooted in the independent charismatic movement which began around 1970. Independent charismatic churches, for the most part, are rooted in classical Pentecostalism. Although the huge ongoing contribution of the Pentecostal movement to the kingdom of God consists of restoring the biblical view of the person and work of the Holy Spirit, ironically two serious flaws crept into their understanding of the operation of spiritual gifts. The first flaw was that the number of spiritual gifts was only nine. The second was the *situational* view of spiritual gifts as over against the *constitutional* view of spiritual gifts.

Let's look at these one at a time.

"The" Nine Gifts of the Spirit

When Pentecostals in the U.S. and in other parts of the world began to be baptized or filled with the Holy Spirit, they began to move in some of the biblical spiritual gifts that were not being used very much in Baptist or Methodist or Presbyterian or Lutheran churches. The gifts that distinguished Pentecostals from the others, such as tongues and interpretation of tongues and prophecy and healings and discernment of spirits and miracles, all seemed to be clustered in the first part of 1 Corinthians 12. Consequently, Pentecostal leaders, quite naturally, focused on that part of Scripture which happened to contain a list of nine spiritual gifts. In their minds, these nine gifts seemed to carry with them a qualitative distinction which set them apart from other activities found in almost all churches, Pentecostal or non-Pentecostal, such as hospitality or administration or evangelism or service or exhortation or mercy or pastoring or giving or leadership or helps.

The upshot of this is that classical Pentecostalism typically speaks of "*the* nine gifts of the Holy Spirit." Most Pentecostals would expect a sermon or a book or a theological essay or a class on the subject of "spiritual gifts" to deal with those nine gifts found in the first part of 1 Corinthians 12. At the same time, the New Testament contains a much longer list than that. Different ones who specialize in spiritual gifts will reach different conclusions as to the total number of spiritual

The gift of apostle, once given by God, becomes a special attribute of the individual that they are responsible to use wisely as good stewards of the grace of God.

gifts, but the list I have used in my newest book on spiritual gifts, *Discovering Your Spiritual Gifts* (Regal Books), contains 28 gifts, each with a concise definition.

How does this relate to George Barna's findings? Many members of apostolic churches have inherited the classical

Pentecostal assumption that there are only nine spiritual gifts. However, a surprisingly large number of church members, even of Pentecostal churches, do not speak in tongues or prophesy or heal the sick or cast out demons, even though they enjoy being around others who do. So when a researcher asks them if they have a spiritual gift, their mind tends to flash through the well-known list of nine, none of which they have to their knowledge, nor are they using them, so they would naturally answer, "No." It may never occur to some of them that they might be ministering in one or more of the other 19 or so spiritual gifts because in their church those gifts are not really awarded the same status as the nine.

In other words, the erroneous conclusion is that if I don't operate in any of the nine gifts of 1 Corinthians 12:8-10, I must not have a spiritual gift.

The Situational View of Spiritual Gifts

The second common flaw in the classical Pentecostal understanding of spiritual gifts relates to their "situational" view of the gifts. Let me explain the difference between the *situational* view of spiritual gifts as over against the *constitutional* view.

The situational view of spiritual gifts assumes that all of the gifts are available to be given to all believers at any time they are needed. In other words, if the "situation" demands that a certain ministry be applied, God will give the individual an appropriate spiritual gift to accomplish that ministry. The individual may rarely, or even never, use that gift again, but it was there for the time it was needed.

The Constitutional View

The constitutional view of spiritual gifts takes more literally the biblical analogy of the body of Christ, with gifted persons expected to function as different members of the body. In the human body, an eye has the attributes of an eye and those are different from the attributes of a kidney or an ear or a tongue. Together they make up the whole body, and eyes are always eyes, kidneys are always kidneys, and so forth. Likewise, in the body of Christ, a person with the gift of evangelist, for example, doesn't just lead one person to Christ here and there, but ministers regularly and powerfully leading unbelievers to Christ. The gift of evangelist, therefore, becomes part of their *constitution*, not just a fleeting ability used in a certain situation. In this view, gifts are given as lifetime possessions, and those who have them are responsible for using them effectively over the long haul.

The constitutional view of spiritual gifts dovetails much more closely with the biblical idea that the church operates like the human body. It also lays the foundation for believers to focus on the gift or gifts that they have been given, developing them and improving in their use as time goes by. The idea that I might have a gift today, but not tomorrow greatly reduces the incentive to spend the time, energy, and money required to develop increasing excellence in that area of ministry.

Explaining Tongues

If I am not mistaken, the situational view of spiritual gifts was developed by early Pentecostal leaders to help explain the phenomenon of tongues. All of a sudden, large numbers of believers in Topeka and Los Angeles and other places started speaking in tongues. As historians of the movement have documented, these early Pentecostal leaders were extremely fervent in their spirits and in biblical power ministries, but not particularly sophisticated in their knowledge of biblical theology. They did know, however, that tongues was one of the biblical spiritual gifts, so they, not surprisingly, assumed that everyone who spoke in tongues must have been given the gift of tongues.

Soon afterward they had to explain the subsequent phenomenon that some who were "baptized in the Holy Spirit" ended up speaking in tongues only once or very infrequently at best. These obviously did not have the ongoing gift of tongues that others apparently had, so the conclusion was that the gift had been given to them for a certain "situation" (i.e., baptism in the Holy Spirit) and perhaps once in a while after that, but not as a permanent possession. This led to what I call the "situational view" of spiritual gifts.

"Roles" vs. "Gifts"

The same phenomena of those days could just as easily, and more biblically, have been explained by the constitutional view of spiritual gifts. It simply entails keeping in mind the distinction between spiritual gifts and Christian roles. There are certain things that every Christian is expected to do just because they are Christians, not because they are gifted. For example, every Christian has a role of being a witness for Christ even though only a few have the gift of evangelism. Every Christian has a role of giving tithes and offerings, but only a few go beyond that with a gift of giving. Every Christian has a role of faith, but some have a spiritual gift of faith. We could go on and on.

The Pentecostal view of tongues (with which some of us have a mild disagreement) is that every believer has a role of speaking in tongues at least once to validate the baptism in the Holy Spirit. This does not have to be attributed to the spiritual gift of tongues, which others obviously have.

The constitutional view of spiritual gifts has the advantage of explaining the phenomena that we see when the Holy Spirit comes in power on individuals and groups while remaining faithful to the strong biblical analogy relating spiritual gifts to the function of the parts of the human body.

The Gift of Apostle

The spiritual gift of apostle is one of the 28 on my list of spiritual gifts. It obviously would be very difficult to understand the gift of apostle through the framework of the situational view. No one would have expected Peter or Paul or John to wake up some days without the gift of apostle. Nor would they have expected the average member of the churches in Ephesus or Rome or Jerusalem to receive the gift of apostle from time to time during their Christian life. No. Both then and now the gift of apostle, once given by God, becomes a special attribute of the individual that they are responsible to use wisely as good stewards of the grace of God.

Repeating what I said previously, knowing that God has entrusted them with the gift of apostle, and not fearing that God may suddenly take that gift from them, is one thing that confers extraordinary authority on true apostles.

Apostolic Assignments

But, beyond that, knowing precisely what their apostolic assignment is raises their confidence in the ministry of the Holy Spirit through them even more.

While all apostles have the gift of apostle, not all have the same assignment. Paul writes, "Now there are diversities of gifts, but the same Spirit. There are differences of ministries, but the same Lord. And there are diversities of activities, but it is the same God who works all in all" (1 Cor. 12:4-6).

Let me explain this by using the gift of evangelist as an example. All evangelists have the gift. But some have a "ministry" of public evangelism, while others have the "ministry" of personal evangelism. Some, of course, have both, but that is beside the point at the moment. Those with a ministry of public evangelism have different "acitvities." Some are city-wide large campaign evangelists; some are itinerant evangelists who travel from church to church; while others exercise their ministry of public evangelism primarily from the pulpit of the church they pastor.

I like to group "ministries" and "activities" under the umbrella of "assignments," or "divine assignments." God gives the gift and He also gives the assignment. The ways that different apostles minister with different assignments is one of the major features of this book. Chapters 6 and 7 will spell this out in detail.

Notes

[1] See "Awareness of Spiritual Gifts Is Changing," News Release from Barna Research Group, Ltd., (Ventura CA), February 5, 2001, pp. 1-2.

CHAPTER FIVE

THE POWER
OF A TITLE

Those of us who have been reading the Bible for years are very familiar with quotes such as, "Paul, called to be an apostle of Jesus Christ through the will of God" (1 Cor. 1:1) or "Paul, an apostle (not from men nor through man, but through Jesus Christ and God the Father who raised Him from the dead)" (Gal. 1:1) or "Paul, an apostle of Jesus Christ by the will of God" (Col. 1:1) or "Peter, an apostle of Jesus Christ" (1 Pet. 1:1) or many other similar statements.

Displaying the Title

What are Paul and Peter doing? They are displaying their title of apostle in a public way.

In fact, Paul specifically declares his apostolic credentials in no fewer than nine of his thirteen epistles. Peter does it in both of his epistles. True, they use other titles along with apostle. Paul calls himself a "servant" in two epistles and Peter in one. Paul also refers to himself as a "prisoner" in his epistle to Philemon. In the other epistles by James, John, and Jude "apostle" is not used. They choose to call themselves "servant" twice and "elder" twice.

In summary, the personal IDs of choice by the authors of the New Testament epistles are:

- ◆ Apostle – 11 times
- ◆ Servant – 5 times
- ◆ Elder – 2 times
- ◆ Prisoner – 1 time

There must be some significance, more than superficial or coincidental, that the title "apostle" is used more than twice as many times as any other title by the leaders who wrote the New Testament epistles. One reason for this, to my way of thinking, is that there is power in the title. For those to whom God has given the spiritual gift of apostle and who have been entrusted with the office of apostle by human representatives of the body of Christ, they apparently are more able to function effectively in their divine assignment with the title "apostle" than they could without it.

Let's think about this.

Jesus Coined the Title

Where did the title "apostle," as applied to Christian leadership, come from? Jesus Himself was the first to use it that way. After praying all one night, the next morning "[Jesus] called His disciples to Him; and from them He chose twelve whom He also named apostles" (Lk. 6:13). This word does not appear in the Old Testament, so it is a term that Jesus specifically coined to apply to certain leaders under the New Covenant. Jesus did not actually invent the word "apostle" because it was already a common secular term in His day. The Greek *apóstolos* means "messenger," or more specifically "messenger with a particular purpose or goal."

New Testament apostles, however, were not just messengers in general, but both Peter and Paul referred to themselves as apostles *of Jesus Christ*. This is important because such a title carries with it a dimension of great authority. It is an ambassadorial authority. It is like Joe Doe, United States Ambassador to Japan. In Japan he is recognized by the title Ambassador Joe Doe, or Mr. Ambassador. In order to fulfill his assignment, the title is essential because it carries the authority that has been personally delegated by the President of the United States. Without the title, Joe Doe is just Joe Doe, and high-level doors do not open to him.

It is reasonable to conclude that Jesus had a specific purpose in choosing the title "apostle" for the twelve whom He considered special among his wider circle of disciples. That is why it seems somewhat odd that the church, for centuries, has tended to steer clear of using the title. It is odd because, as I hinted in Chapter 2, we seem to be comfortable in using titles for other governmental or foundational offices found in Ephesians 4:11. For pastors we have no problem with "Pastor Mike" or "Reverend Johnson." "Evangelist Billy Graham" sounds o.k. People often refer to me as "Dr. Wagner," to acknowledge that I am a teacher, and I accept that even though I

balk at flaunting it. I am secure in the fact that I have earned
my Ph.D., but in personal conversation I prefer "Peter."

Breaking Boundaries

"Doctor" is one thing, but how about *"Apostle* So-and-so?" I
admit that it still sounds a bit strange, even to me. It breaks
boundaries. It takes us out of our comfort zones. Even so, it
is part and parcel of the new paradigm that God has provided
for the church. I am thoroughly convinced that one of the
things the Spirit is saying to the churches these days is that we
must get the biblical government of the church in place and
that an important part of the process is to begin to use the title
"apostle" when appropriate.

Actually, the New Testament uses the term "apostle" much
more than it uses the other Ephesians 4:11 titles which today's
church leaders seem to feel more comfortable with. Here is
the count of appearances of the words in the New Testament:

♦ Apostle – 74
♦ Teacher – 14
♦ Prophet – 8
♦ Evangelist – 3
♦ Pastor – 3

The Adjective Is Not Enough

For a number of our more tentative Christian leaders, the adjective "apostolic" is acceptable, while the noun "apostle" is
avoided. They speak of "apostolic leadership" or "apostolic
churches" or "apostolic ministry" with the implication that by

doing so they are describing apostles. At times they even make the adjective a noun and refer to "the apostolic." In my opinion, this choice weakens considerably the biblical church government that God is desiring to put into place. In fact, I looked up the word "apostolic" in the concordance, and I couldn't find it in my New King James Version!

There are at least two reasons why some prefer the unbiblical "apostolic" to the biblical "apostle." The first reason is attached to some who do not believe that there are any

---

I am thoroughly convinced that one of the things the Spirit is saying to the churches these days is that we must get the biblical government of the church in place and that an important part of the process is to begin to use the title "apostle" when appropriate.

---

apostles in the church today, and the second is attached to some who do. Let's look at them.

There are those who use the adjective and not the noun in order to help argue the point that the title "apostle" was discontinued in the church after the first two hundred years or so of church history. In Chapter 1, I mentioned that the American Assemblies of God had taken this position through an official denominational "white paper." The paper attempts to argue that some people (like me!) are wrongly interpreting Scriptures such as 1 Corinthians 12:28 and Ephesians 2:20 and 4:11. It attributes "the problematic teaching that present-day offices of apostles and prophets should govern church ministries at all levels" to "persons with an independent spirit and an exaggerated estimate of their importance in the kingdom of God." Then the paper concludes by choosing to use the adjective and not the noun: "We affirm that there are and ought to be, apostolic- and prophetic-type ministries in the Church, without individuals being identified as filling such an office."[1]

An Entry-Level Approach

On the other hand, some who *do* believe that we have apostles in churches today prefer to use "apostolic" instead of "apostle" because they feel that the adjective is less threatening and therefore that it provides a more entry-level approach to those who might be seeking. This is commendable, and there might be wisdom in so doing, at least for a limited time. An example of this is the first widely-circulated book on the apostolic movement published in Australia, *The 21st Century Church Out There*, edited by Ben Gray (CityHarvest Publications). In that book, only the adjective is used. However, the second Australian book, *The Apostolic Revolution* by David Cartledge (Paraclete Institute) overcomes the reluctance of the first and uses the noun "apostle" freely. This, along with many other factors including key apostolic conferences convened by Ben Gray, have brought Australia to the place of, arguably, the most advanced nation *as a nation* in understanding and applying apostolic government to church life.

I think that John Eckhardt, in his book *Leadershift* (Crusaders Ministries), makes a very good point. He is a strong advocate of using the title, and for years he has cordially accepted the designation, Apostle John Eckhardt. In his book he argues that when the government of the church is in place under one or more apostles, then every church can be an apostolic church, every believer should be apostolic, every teacher should be apostolic, every evangelist should be apostolic, every pastor should be apostolic, and so on. If this is the case, then it is clear that the adjective "apostolic" has its place, but not as a substitute for "apostle" as a noun.

Is "Apostle" a Red Flag?

The propriety of using the title "apostle" is being vigorously discussed wherever church leaders desire to move a bit closer to the cutting edge. I'm not going to mention names at this point, but I was interested in reading a dialogue on the Internet recently that went something like this:

Person A: "A pastoral vision fails to provide a large enough foundation for the church. It wants to take care of the sheep we have. An evangelistic vision focuses outward primarily, which is important. However it can fail to nurture the sheep we have. It is necessary to have an apostolic vision of the kingdom of God in place in order to support the superstructure God wants to build."

Person B: "I agree whole-heartedly. However, I've shied away from using the title and have sought to focus more on the function—mostly because the language means so many things to so many different people."

Person A: "Some people put themselves forward as 'apostles,' when they aren't. Others function as apostles, but have no desire for the title. It is a 'red flag' term for so many people."

These two individuals are agreeing that a danger of using the title "apostle" is that some might take offense. It might precipitate disunity in the body of Christ. I think that they are making an accurate observation, but I also think that their fears are not altogether justified. I am afraid that some will be so consumed with preserving the status quo that Christian unity actually becomes an end in itself. When this happens it is very difficult to make changes and advance the kingdom of God, especially when God is trying to form a new wineskin.

This might well have been the case with the leaders back in the post-World War II apostolic movement. Bill Hamon, in his exciting new book, *The Coming Saints Movement*, says, "The restorational Latter Rain movement teaching concerning apostles and prophets never affected much of the Church world because those called to these offices were never given, nor accepted the titles of apostle and prophet."[2] Unfortunately they either did not understand the power of a title or they caved in to some of the strong opposition that was being aimed at their movement in those days.

However, having said that, I must also say that I have found much less opposition to accepting the gift and office of apostle than I had originally expected. We went public with the idea of the New Apostolic Reformation with the National Symposium on the Postdenominational Church at Fuller Seminary in 1996. To my knowledge, no national-level wave of opposition has materialized since. Consequently, the risk that the title of apostle could be a "red flag" might not be as much of a risk as some imagine.

Apostles Are Not Made Overnight

One of the most insightful books on apostolic leadership is *Apostles* by Bill Scheidler (CityBible Publishing). Two of his chapters contain a personal interview with Dick Iverson, the founder of one of America's foremost apostolic networks, Ministers Fellowship International (MFI) out of Portland, Oregon. Dick Iverson is one who has functioned for years as an apostle, but who, until recently, resisted accepting the title. One reason for this was that he had seen the term abused so much in the past. Some people were even suspected of calling themselves apostles for their own enrichment. Unwise prophets would at times aid and abet this by off-the-cuff prophecies that a certain person was an apostle.

Iverson tells this story: "I had a young man in his twenties in my office this morning. He said that he was an apostle, and that when he goes back to his homeland, he expects they will receive him as an apostle. Well, that may happen twenty years from now. But for him to go back and somehow expect to be a recognized apostle overnight...I personally don't think that will happen."[3]

How is a person recognized as an apostle? There is no single agreed-upon process, but for Dick Iverson to agree that someone like the young man in his office is really an apostle, it would have to be affirmed four ways: (1) The apostle needs to know God's call personally; (2) The leadership of his own local church needs to affirm it; (3) The congregation of the apostle's local church needs to agree, and (4) Those whom the apostle has established and grounded in the faith need to recognize him.[4]

Struggling with the Title

I like the way that Apostle Trevor Newport of England describes his experience of coming to terms with being an apostle.[5] Newport, now a member of the International Coalition of Apostles, had been a pastor for 14 years before he began to hear the Lord say, "I have made you an apostle—please accept it." This was difficult because he had already decided never to call himself an apostle. He struggled with the issue for three years.

A breaking point came when he sat under Colin Urquhart, a well-known British apostle, at a pastors' conference. Urquhart said, "I have been struggling for 3 years with accepting the apostolic call." That got Trevor's attention. After the conference, Trevor Newport prayed and simply said, "O.K., Lord, I accept the apostolic call, whatever it means."

Did accepting the title of "apostle" convey power?

The Power of a Title

"Two weeks later," Newport says, "I was in a prayer meeting with about 8 others when, all of a sudden, the presence of God filled the room. We were all affected by it and could not move or speak. All I could move were my eyes! Then I saw three angels come down from heaven with Jesus in the midst. The three angels stayed outside of the door of our prayer room and Jesus came in on His own. He came straight up to me and said these words: 'Hi, Trev, it's your brother Jesus here. I've

come to tell you that your ministry is just about to start. Bye!'
I then saw Him join the three angels and go back to heaven. It
was awesome! I did not realize what was happening or the
effect that it would have on my ministry.

"Up until that time I only had one church which was still
in its pioneer stage. Then, from that visitation on, pastors
kept calling me and asking me if they could come under my
covering. I had not announced anything to anyone about that!

"Within two years, Life Changing Ministries had grown
to 8 churches in the UK, 17 churches in Sri Lanka, 25 churches
in Nepal, 1 church in Japan, many churches in India, and 1
church in Colorado. I have now ministered in 50 countries
and written 16 books."

Three Years Three Times

When I found that both Trevor Newport and Colin Urquhart
had struggled for three years to accept the title of apostle once
they began to hear God about it, I retraced my own experience
and found that, surprisingly enough, my process took three
years as well. The first prophetic word I received that I had
the anointing of an apostle came through Cindy Jacobs in July
1995 and the second through an intercessor, Margaret Moberly,
two months later. I had no idea as to what I should do about it
at that time. Early in 1998 God spoke to me again, this time in
a public meeting through Prophet Jim Stevens. I then had no
doubt that I would have to go public, but still I was not yet
ready.

My problem was that I didn't know what kind of an apostle
I was. It was only later that year that I began to understand
different kinds of apostolic spheres. Once I could define my

sphere of authority, I was ready to accept the title and receive the divine power that accompanied it. I'll explain how my understanding was clarified in the next chapter.

Before I do that, however, I should add one more note concerning timing. In a European Apostolic Summit that I convened in Oslo in 2002, I took an informal poll to see how long it had required for European apostles to move from the point where they first knew inwardly that they were apostles, until they became comfortable with using and allowing the term to be used for themselves in public. Of 25 apostles who responded, not one had accepted the title in less than three years. The results were, three years: nine apostles; four years: three apostles; five years: two apostles; and six or more years: eleven apostles. This should go a long way toward neutralizing the frequently heard criticism that apostles tend to be insecure individuals with an insatiable appetite for titles.

Notes

1   See "Endtime Revival—Spirit-Led and Spirit Controlled: A Response Paper to Resolution 16," subsection "Deviant Teachings Disapproved," issued by the General Presbytery of the General Council of the Assemblies of God, August 11, 2000.
2   Bill Hamon, *The Coming Saints Movement* (Santa Rosa Beach, FL: Christian International, 2002), p. 139.
3   Bill Scheidler, *Apostles: The Fathering Servant* (Portland OR: CityBible Publishing, 2001), p. 191.
4   Ibid., pp. 181-182.
5   This account is excerpted from personal correspondence from Trevor Newport to the author, January 26, 2001.

CHAPTER SIX

THREE BROAD APOSTOLIC SPHERES OF MINISTRY

Throughout this book I have reiterated time and again that the major characteristic that distinguishes apostles from other members of the body of Christ is their extraordinary authority. The New Apostolic Reformation is the most radical change in the way of doing church since the Protestant Reformation, and of all the different changes that can be listed, Number One is *the amount of spiritual authority delegated by the Holy Spirit to individuals.* I am aware that I have said this before, but it is well worth repeating.

Biblical Examples

Let's look at some biblical examples of what it means for an apostle to exercise authority:

♦ *Apostle Peter:* "There were also false prophets among the people, even as there will be false teachers among you, who will secretly bring in destructive heresies, even denying the Lord who bought them, and bring on themselves swift destruction" (2 Pet. 2:1). This is strong language!

♦ *Apostle James:* "Therefore I judge that we should not trouble those from among the Gentiles who are turning to God" (Acts 15:19). This was one of the most decisive apostolic declarations ever made. I will come back to James and the Council of Jerusalem later.

♦ *Apostle John:* "If anyone comes to you and does not bring this doctrine, do not receive him into your house nor greet him; for he who greets him shares in his evil deeds" (2 Jn. 10). John is very sure of himself and of his teaching!

♦ *Apostle Paul:* "O foolish Galatians! Who has bewitched you that you should not obey the truth...Are you so foolish? Having begun in the Spirit, are you now being made perfect by the flesh?" (Gal. 3:1,3). Paul has few inhibitions when he severely reprimands certain fellow believers. In another place he sounds quite a bit like the quote from John just above: "And if anyone does not obey our word in this epistle, note that person and do not keep company with him, that he may be ashamed" (2 Thess. 3:14). Apparently anyone who disagrees with Paul is in serious trouble!

Apostolic Spheres Determine Apostolic Authority

Read through the Book of Acts and the epistles and you will see many similar quotes from apostles. There is little room to question that they possessed extraordinary authority. But let's go one step further. Exactly where did this apostolic authority function? It did not function everywhere. It only functioned within the *apostolic sphere (or spheres)* of each individual apostle.

Take, for example, Paul's relationship to the believers in the city of Corinth. It is a good case in point because in the church at Corinth there happened to be some outspoken believers who actually questioned Paul's apostolic authority. They had decided that they were not going to submit to him. Big mistake! Paul writes 2 Corinthians 10 and 11 in order to address them directly.

Paul's Critics

What were these critics saying about Paul? Four things:

1. *Paul was ugly and boring!* ("'For his letters,' they say, 'are weighty and powerful, but his bodily presence is weak, and his speech contemptible.'" [2 Cor. 10:10]).

2. *Paul was not as good as the real apostles!* (In response, Paul had to say: "For I consider that I am not at all inferior to the most eminent apostles" [2 Cor. 11:5]).

3. *Paul was money hungry!* ("Did I commit sin in abasing myself that you might be exalted, because I preached the gospel of God to you free of charge? I robbed other churches, taking wages from them to minister to you. And when I was present with you, and in need, I was a burden to no one, for what was lacking the brethren who came from Macedonia supplied. And in everything I kept myself from being burdensome to you, and so I will keep myself" [2 Cor. 11:7-9]).

4. *Paul was a self-appointed apostle, and therefore he had no authority!* ("For even if I should boast somewhat about our authority, which the Lord gave us for edification and not for your destruction, I shall not be ashamed" [2 Cor. 10:8]).

"Boasting" about Authority

Paul, not surprisingly, was considerably upset by these accusations. He addressed them directly in the quotes that I just listed. But he also addressed them more broadly by explaining the concept of apostolic spheres. Paul not only knew that he had extraordinary authority, but he went so far as to "boast" about it several times in 1 Corinthians 10 and 11. For example, in 2 Corinthians 10:8, Paul says that he "boasts" about his authority, quickly adding that his authority comes only from God. The Greek word for "boasting" means to glory in the acts of God. Therefore, Paul was not exalting himself, he was exalting God, who had chosen to give him divine *exousía* or authority.

Paul was acutely aware that the apostolic authority he had been given by God could only be exercised in certain places at certain times. He was not an apostle to the whole body of Christ everywhere. He wrote to the Corinthians: "Am I not an apostle? Am I not free? Have I not seen Jesus

---

Apostles have awesome, divinely-imparted authority, but outside their God-determined sphere they don't have any more authority than any other member of the body of Christ!

Christ our Lord? Are you not my work in the Lord? *If I am not an apostle to others*, yet doubtless I am to you" (1 Cor. 9:1-2). I italicized that phrase because in it Paul admits that he is not an apostle to everybody. For example, he was not an apostle in Alexandria or in Jerusalem or in Rome. But he definitely *was* an apostle in Corinth as well as in Ephesus and Philippi and Galatia and many other places which constituted his spheres.

"Boasting" within Spheres

Paul applies his "boasting" about his divine authority to specific spheres in 2 Corinthians 10 and 11. Here are two quotes from these chapters in which I am italicizing the several appearances of "boasting" and "spheres."

"We, however, will not *boast* beyond measure, but within the limits of the *sphere* which God appointed us—a *sphere* which especially includes you. [In other words, the Corinthians are under Paul's apostolic authority because they are included in his God-given sphere.] For we are not extending ourselves beyond our *sphere* (thus not reaching you), for it was to you that we came with the gospel of Christ; not *boasting* of things beyond measure, that is, in other men's labors, but having hope, that as your faith is increased, we shall be greatly enlarged by you in our *sphere*" (2 Cor. 10:13-15).

"As the truth of Christ is in me, no one shall stop me from this *boasting* in the regions of Achaia" (2 Cor. 11:10). Achaia was the Roman province which included Corinth, clearly one of Paul's assigned spheres.

Limits of Apostolic Authority

Let me summarize this with one of the more important thoughts of this book: *Apostles have awesome, divinely-imparted authority, but outside their God-determined sphere they don't have any more authority than any other member of the body of Christ!*

I feel this is important because, if I am not mistaken, many leaders in today's apostolic movement could do a little better in their practical understanding of the general principle of apostolic spheres as well as a knowledge of what these spheres actually are and how they can be defined. As a result, some apostolic ministry not only tends to be misunderstood, but it can actually be rejected by some who have experienced attempts to apply it in the wrong spheres.

As I detailed in Chapter 4, all apostles, by definition, have the spiritual gift of apostle. However not all apostles have the same ministry or activity. This statement is an application of 1 Corinthians 12:4-6: "Now there are diversities of gifts, but the same Spirit. There are differences of ministries but the same Lord. And there are diversities of activities, but it is the same God who works all in all."

Apostolic Ministries and Activities

What, then, are the different "ministries" and "activities" that involve those who have the gift of apostle?

As I attempt to answer this question, readers would do well to keep in mind that my research methodology is not philo-sophical or theological (in the classical sense) or exegetical or revelational, but rather phenomenological. I will necessarily be employing terms which are not found in the Bible because I believe it is not only necessary to use the *Word* of God, but also to combine with it accurate observation of the *works* of God. I am not approaching this so much from the question of what God *ought* to do as much as what God *is* actually doing. What the Spirit has said to the churches is one thing, but what the Spirit is actually saying now is another.

In the next chapter I will propose a more detailed taxonomy of apostolic spheres, but for now let's look at the three broad-est categories of apostolic ministry that have become clear at the present time. I say "present time" because further research might turn up more categories or might demand refinement of these, but they do at least provide us a starting point. My names for these are "vertical apostles," "horizontal apostles," and "marketplace apostles."

Vertical Apostles

Most apostles are vertical apostles. They lead networks of churches or ministries or individuals who look to the apostle for spiritual "covering" and who are comfortable under the authority of that particular apostle. A biblical prototype of a vertical apostle is the apostle Paul. Many churches looked to Paul for their apostolic covering, as did individuals such as Timothy and Titus.

When I compiled my book *The New Apostolic Churches* (Regal Books), I invited eighteen apostles to write first-person accounts of their own apostolic networks. They were all vertical apostles. They were "vertical" in the sense that each of them had a network of which they were at the top. For each of them, the primary apostolic sphere in which their authority received a divine anointing was their particular network. Vertical apostles are so common that, back in those days, it had never even occurred to me that there might be other kinds of apostles.

Horizontal Apostles

Horizontal apostles, unlike vertical apostles, do not have churches or ministries or individuals under them for whom they furnish spiritual "covering." Rather, they serve peer-level leaders in helping them to connect with each other for different purposes. Our best biblical example is James of Jerusalem who convened the Council of Jerusalem in order to deal with the issue as to whether Gentiles needed to be circumcised and become "Jews" in order to be saved.

It is good to keep in mind that this James was not one of the original twelve apostles. There were two apostles named James among the original twelve. One we know very little about, and the other was a son of Zebedee and a member of

Jesus' inner circle of Peter, James and John. That James was killed by Herod in Acts 12. This James was the blood brother of Jesus, a son of Mary and Joseph. He was a leader in the church of Jerusalem.

I mention this because the apostles who came to Jerusalem at James' invitation were vertical apostles such as Peter and John and Paul and Matthew and Apollo and Barnabas and Thomas and the rest. I could not prove this, but I have a strong suspicion that none of those vertical apostles could have successfully called the Jerusalem Council. Vertical apostles are not usually inclined to seek each other out and spend time with each other, especially if they don't like each other very much. It took a horizontal apostle like James to bring these peers together.

Issuing an Apostolic Declaration

James had full apostolic authority in the Jerusalem Council. After the apostles who were in attendance had said what they felt they needed to say about the issue of Gentile circumcision, James did not take a vote or form a commission to study the matter further or convene an executive council. He issued an apostolic declaration: "Therefore, I judge that we should not trouble those from among the Gentiles who are turning to God" (Acts 15:19). Notice the use of the first person singular in his statement. This is an apostle doing what an apostle is supposed to do.

Notice also the response of the other, quite renowned, apostles who were present. They gladly received the authoritative word from James. "It pleased the apostles and the el-

ders and the whole church" (Acts 15:22). James had unbelievable authority because he was functioning in his God-given
sphere as a horizontal apostle.

However, when the apostles moved on from the Council
of Jerusalem, they were no longer under James' authority. He
did not continue to "cover" them because he was not a vertical apostle like they were.

Marketplace Apostles

A third significant broad sphere of apostolic ministry is marketplace apostles. The vertical and horizontal apostles that I
have just described do their ministry primarily in what could
be called the "nuclear church." Marketplace apostles do their
ministry primarily in the "extended church." Just as sociolo-
gists distinguish between the "nuclear family" and the "extended family," I believe that we can do the same with the
church.

Our biblical prototypes of marketplace apostles are Luke
and Lydia of Philippi. I will go into more detail about marketplace apostles in Chapter 8 when I deal with the role of
apostles in social transformation.

Spheres Are Crucial

Apostles can never become everything that God wants them
to be unless they are fully conscious of the sphere or spheres
of ministry to which God has assigned each one of them. A
good beginning point for understanding apostolic spheres is
distinguishing between vertical apostles, horizontal apostles,

and marketplace apostles. But, particularly for those who are leaders, there are several other subcategories of spheres which will give us further direction in knowing how we all fit together into the body of Christ. I will suggest some of these in the next chapter.

CHAPTER SEVEN

MANY APOSTLES, MANY SPHERES

In the last chapter I introduced the terms "vertical apostle," "horizontal apostle," and "marketplace apostle." Now I am going to suggest perhaps a dozen other terms that might also be applied to different kinds of apostles. As I set out to do this, I am aware that some readers may begin to complain that I am overcomplicating the situation. While I understand that such a thing could well be possible, in my mind it turns out just the opposite. I am attempting to *simplify* things, at least for those of us who are specialists.

Specialists Need Detail

I am willing to admit that this chapter may actually be more suited to those who desire to be specialists in the area of apostolic ministry than to believers in general. It brings to mind certain taxonomies of livestock as an illustration of some of the benefits that detail can actually provide. Both Doris and I are dairy farmers, so one of our personal areas of expertise is dairy cattle. Doris was a member of the New York State 4-H dairy cattle judging team. I have my undergraduate degree in dairy production, and I was on the Rutgers University dairy cattle judging team. Thus, we both probably qualify as specialists in that relatively small area of interest.

When Doris and I are driving down the highway and we see animals in a field, we do not react the way that probably 95 percent of other motorists react. The great majority would say, "Look at the cows!" They, thereby, display their ability to tell cows from horses or sheep, which is admittedly all that most people need. A few of them might also observe that they are dairy cattle as over against beef cattle. If we saw them, however, we would invariably say, "Look at the Holsteins!" Unlike non-specialists, it is very important to Doris and me to know that at that moment we are not looking at Guernseys or Ayrshires or Jerseys or Brown Swiss.

Applying this to apostolic ministry, much of the Christian public would admittedly do well just to be able to tell the difference between apostles and prophets. That is as far as they probably need to go. However, leaders who are closely involved with apostles, apostolic churches, apostolic ministries, or apostolic teaching will be grateful for, let's call it, this "apostolic taxonomy."

Apostles Are Servants

Back in Chapter 1, I mentioned that a pioneer movement of apostles sprang up after World War II, but some mistakes were made and many of those movements turned out to be relatively short-lived. One of the mistakes of some of the apostles was to allow themselves to become overly authoritarian. My friend, Leo Lawson of Morning Star International, has contrasted what he calls "World War II" apostles with the "Microsoft apostles" who are more characteristic of today's New Apostolic Reformation. Microsoft apostles strive to be much more relational than dictatorial. This, very importantly, allows them to function more as servants than otherwise might be possible.

Can apostles really be servants? I would answer this question with the bold suggestion that no one can actually be a true apostle at all unless they are also a servant. Let me explain.

The question is not surprising. After all, in the Bible apostles are labeled with glowing terms such as "first" (1 Cor. 12:28) and "foundation" (Eph. 2:20). Among all of the disciples that Jesus had, the apostles constituted the most elite group. I have described in detail the unbelievable authority that characterizes apostles. How could someone as exalted as an apostle turn out to be a genuine servant as well?

Apostolic Leadership and Servanthood

Two of Jesus' apostles, James and John, could answer that question by experience. At one point they wanted to exalt themselves. They wanted to be Jesus' chief lieutenants in the Kingdom. Jesus rebuked them for this and used the opportunity to teach them, as well as the rest of His apostles, a profound lesson on servant leadership. He first told them, negatively, that apostles must not be like Gentiles and "lord it over [other people]" (Mark 10:42). Jesus then goes to the positive side and says, "Whoever desires to become great among you shall be your servant" (Mark 10:43). Apostolic leadership, as contrasted to secular leadership, is based on servanthood. There is no other way to get it.

Notice that Jesus does not say there is anything wrong with wanting to "become great." However, He does say that in the kingdom of God apostolic leadership does not come through coercion or self-imposition. It cannot be demanded. It must be earned. If the litmus test of an apostle is that he or she has followers, those followers must perceive the apostle to be their servant before they will decide to follow.

Keep in mind that the only opinion that really counts as to whether a given apostle is a servant or not is that of the apostle's followers. Individuals in other apostolic spheres may get on a certain apostle's case and deny that he or she behaves like a servant. But their opinion has little weight as long as those in the apostle's own sphere do perceive him or her to be their servant. Servanthood consists of the fact that the followers believe the decisions the apostle makes are ultimately for their benefit. Because of that, they like the decisions and they stick with the apostle.

Foundational vs. Reformational Apostles

My friend, Roger Mitchell of England, once suggested to me that most apostles will fit into one of two categories of primary apostolic characteristics: "foundational apostles" or "reformational apostles."

Foundational apostles are those who move out to take new territory. They are boundary breakers. They color outside of the lines. Paul would have been a foundational apostle. He said, "I have made it my aim to preach the gospel, not where Christ was named, lest I should build on another man's foun-

---

If the litmus test of an apostle is that he or she has followers, those followers must perceive the apostle to be their servant before they will decide to follow.

---

dation" (Rom. 15:20). Paul planted the church in Corinth and later wrote back to the believers there, "As a wise master builder I have laid the foundation, and another builds on it" (1 Cor. 3:10). Well-known foundational apostles would include Patrick of Ireland and William Carey and Hudson Taylor and many others.

Reformational apostles, on the other hand, move in to regain territory once claimed by foundational apostles, but mostly or partially lost over time due to negative spiritual forces. John, who took over the church in Ephesus which Paul had planted might serve as a biblical example. Others, who have made a mark on Christian history, would include Martin Luther and John Wesley and Jonathan Edwards, and many others.

Eight Apostolic "Activities"

"Foundational" and "reformational" are generalized terms. Now, let's be much more specific. I am going to suggest four sub-categories of vertical apostles and four more of horizontal apostles. In all probability, both foundational apostles and reformational apostles could be found in each of these eight kinds of apostolic activity.

I call these "activities" because I am using 1 Corinthians 12:4-6, where it speaks of "gifts," "ministries," and "activities" as a framework, admitting, as I do it, that I could be stretching the application of that particular passage a bit at this point. Even so, I like to think that under the "gift" of apostle, which all apostles have, some have different "ministries" including vertical, horizontal, and marketplace, and some have different "activities" embracing these eight sub-categories.

Recognizing these eight apostolic activities could go a long way in preventing the frustration of what we might call "pseudo authority." It will help apostles more clearly recognize the spheres to which God has assigned them and within which God has delegated to them apostolic authority. Hopefully, it will also help to prevent apostles from attempting to exercise authority outside of their sphere or spheres. Trouble is just around the corner when one apostle steps into another apostle's sphere and begins to take over. This ends up in an exhibition of pseudo authority. Recognizing where one sphere of authority ends and another begins should help keep this from happening.

Four "Activities" of Vertical Apostles

The chief distinguishing characteristic of vertical apostles in general is that they are at the head of an ongoing organization of some type. They are at the top—the rest are somewhere underneath. The apostles are not at the top because they have successfully climbed the corporate ladder of some hierarchy. They are at the top because the relationships which they have built with the others demand that they lead. They are servants. They serve the others by leading them and by exercising their apostolic authority on behalf of their followers. Vertical apostles provide a 24/7 spiritual "covering" for others in their network. They consider themselves successful if they are somehow able to help those who follow them become everything that God wants them to be.

There are four sub-categories or "activities" of vertical apostles:

1. Ecclesiastical Apostles

If somebody did a study on this, it would probably turn out that ecclesiastical apostles constitute the largest number of all the categories of apostolic activities. This is where the apostle Paul would have fit. Ecclesiastical apostles are given a sphere which includes a number of churches, and some expand this a bit to include certain parachurch ministries as well. When we currently use the term "apostolic network," most of the time we have an ecclesiastical network in mind. Whereas denominations were once upon a time the new wineskins into which God was pouring new wine, apostolic networks now appear to be the new wineskins.

The pastors of the churches and leaders of parachurch ministries within the network look to the apostle for their spiritual covering. Frequently pastors receive their ordination to ministry at the hands of the apostle. The apostle is their covering, their spiritual father or mother. Ecclesiastical apostles have permission to speak into the lives of the pastors, both for encouragement and for rebuke when necessary. Ordinarily this covenant relationship is sealed and perpetuated by the pastors' giving a tithe of their personal income to the apostle. They trust the discretion of the apostles to use the money wisely both to meet their own personal needs and for the advance of the kingdom of God.

Some better-known examples of ecclesiastical apostles today would include Larry Kreider of DOVE Christian Fellowship International based in Ephrata, Pennsylvania (98 churches in 9 nations), Bill Hamon of Christian International based in Santa Rosa Beach, Florida (405 churches and 605 ministries in 20 nations), Naomi Dowdy of Global Leadership Network based in Singapore (490 churches in 17 nations), Enoch Adeboye of Nigeria (over 5,000 churches, 3,500 in Nigeria and 1,500 in 50 other countries), and thousands of others like them.

2. Apostolic Team Members

Most apostles develop a leadership team of one kind or another to support them in their apostolic ministry. Members of that team frequently include spouses, prophets, administrators, close friends, financial supporters, and others. Generally speaking, however, one apostle heads the network. A few, nevertheless, choose to bring onto their leadership team other peer-level apostles. This requires a special kind of "Microsoft apostle," but when it can be done it greatly expands the possibility of including more churches in the network.

In my book, *Churchquake!* I go into considerable detail explaining why there is a numerical limit to the number of churches that can participate in a healthy ecclesiastical apostolic network.[1] This is based on the axiom that apostolic networks, as contrasted to denominations, are held together by personal relationships instead of by legal, bureaucratic, organizational designs. It is essential, therefore, that the leader of the network, the apostle, maintain a personal relationship with the pastors of all the churches of the network. Depending on a set of variables, the range of churches in which this can happen is something between 50 and 150 churches.

This range would apply to networks under one apostle. But if networks are headed by an apostolic team, the more apostles on the team, the more churches can be brought into this relational structure. To my knowledge, the forerunner in implementing the concept of an apostolic team is Morning Star International under Rice Broocks. Jim Laffoon, who serves as a prophet (not an apostle) on the Morning Star apostolic team has explained this concept in his excellent book, *A Divine Alliance*. He argues that "If the one-apostle-per-network model is the only model of building apostolic networks perpetuated, the ability of the body of Christ to advance the kingdom of God around the world could be impaired."[2] He then goes on to show how Jesus, Peter, and Paul all employed apostolic teams.

The apostles whom Rice Broocks, the unquestionable first among equals in Morning Star, has invited to join him on his team include Phil Bonasso of Torrance, California,

Steve Murrell of the Philippines, Greg Ball of Austin, Texas, Ron Lewis of Charlotte, North Carolina, and Paul Daniel of South Africa. In the way I am defining things, those five would not be pure and simple ecclesiastical apostles like Rice Broocks is, but they would be apostolic team members.

3. Functional Apostles

Functional apostles do not oversee or provide apostolic covering to a number of churches. Rather, they have been given apostolic authority over individuals or groups who operate within a certain kind of specialized ministry. Their followers may be under a personal covering of another leader. For example they might be members of a local church and, naturally, accountable to their pastor. Still, in a particular area of ministry or with a particular affinity group, they might also look to a functional apostle for direction, discipling, and accountability for excellence in that area.

Jane Hansen of Aglow International would be an example. She is a recognized apostle, a member of the International Coalition of Apostles. She is a member of a local church and accountable to her pastor. Yet she gives apostolic oversight to one of the world's most prominent organizations of Christian women. Fifty state Aglow presidents look to her for covering in the United States, and so do national Presidents of 150 other nations of the world. The covering applies to their activities related to Aglow, although it might also be a bit broader in certain individual cases.

Another example is Chris Hayward of Cleansing Stream, also a member of ICA. He has done more to set in place deliverance ministry teams in local churches than anyone else to my knowledge. Over 2,500 churches in the U.S.A., and over 500 churches in 22 other countries are actively offering the Cleansing Stream Seminar. A significant number of these churches have at least one and sometimes multiple deliverance ministry teams developed and functioning under the covering of the local church pastor. Team members and leaders first experience the Seminar and Retreat themselves, then ultimately enter the 2nd year Cleansing Stream Discipleship Program. Leaders of this enormous international movement look to Chris Hayward as their functional apostle, even though many have not as yet become used to using the title.

I could mention others such as Loren Cunningham providing apostolic leadership to Youth with a Mission or Ché Ahn over The Call, arguably the most dynamic youth movement of our day, or many others. They are all functional apostles, in that role not over churches or pastors but over different dynamic movements which help advance the kingdom of God.

4. Congregational Apostles

My primary area of academic expertise happens to be the field of church growth. Years of extensive research have brought me to the conclusion that there are only two predictable numerical barriers to the growth of a local church, namely the 200 barrier and the 700-800 barrier, the numbers indicating "active members" however that may be defined. Something like 90 percent of American churches are under 200, and another 7 to 8 percent would be between 200 and 700-800. That leaves 2, possibly 3, percent over the 700-800 range.

Crossing each one of these barriers, with the church continuing to grow on the other side, is more than anything else a function of leadership. Although many factors enter the equation for breaking the 200 barrier,[3] the major change in leadership involves the pastor agreeing to become a "rancher" instead of a "shepherd." A shepherd offers one-on-one care to all parishioners, and this model, when other conditions are right, can get a church up to 200. But over 200 the pastor needs to begin delegating pastoral care to others. The rancher does not personally care for the sheep, but he or she is responsible for making sure it gets done. Due to the fact that this change in ministry style is next to impossible for most pastors to initiate and for most congregations to accept, 90 percent of churches will remain under the 200 barrier.

A few, however, will cross 200, but plateau out somewhere on this side of 700-800. Again, moving beyond 700-800 requires a special kind of leader. Back in 1980, America's foremost parish consultant, Lyle Schaller, suggested that a church of over 700 could accurately be described as a "minidenomination."[4] In 1999, Gary McIntosh, another highly regarded church growth expert, used secular labels to describe pastoral leadership of several sizes of churches, calling pastors of churches over 800 "president." His final category was churches of over 2,000 in which the pastor would be seen as "chairman."[5]

With these figures somewhere in the back of my mind, I was once discussing leadership roles with my pastor, Ted Haggard. Our church, New Life Church of Colorado Springs, was at that time over 6,000 and growing (at this writing it is over 8,000). By that time I had begun teaching on and writing about apostles. Suddenly it dawned on me that the best term for the leader of a "minidenomination" like New Life Church was not "president" or "chairman," but rather "apostle." To use new wineskin terminology, a "mini apostolic network" might be a better description than "minidenomination." Given the fact that the average church in America has a Sunday attendance of around 85, an attendance of 6,000 would be the equivalent of something like 70 churches, a decent-sized apostolic network in itself.

As is the case with most of us, Ted did not want to accept the title "apostle" at first, but now he is comfortable with it, and he has even started an ecclesiastical apostolic network, The Association of Life-Giving Churches. His pastoral leadership role would clearly fit under this category of "congregational apostle." As frequently happens, the church that the congregational apostle pastors, in this case New Life Church, also becomes the anchor church for the vertical apostolic network.

Four "Activities" of Horizontal Apostles

As I said in the last chapter, a major distinguishing characteristic of horizontal, as over against vertical, apostles is that the horizontal apostles do not ordinarily provide spiritual covering or direct ongoing personal accountability to those to whom they minister. Their anointing is to bring together peers of one kind or another to accomplish certain purposes better than they could separately.

There are four sub-categories or "activities" of horizontal apostles:

1. Convening Apostles

This is the sub-category of apostles that I can write about in the first person. I see myself, much like James of Jerusalem, as a horizontal apostle with "convening" as my primary activity. Those of us who serve as convening apostles have been given an anointing to call together peer-level Christian leaders who minister in a defined field on a regular basis. We have the ability to form relational organizations for specific purposes as God directs. For several years now I have been doing this, and here is a list of the groups I am currently "apostling:"

♦ *Apostolic Council for Educational Accountability (ACEA).* This was formed to provide the educational institutions in the New Apostolic Reformation a creative functional substitute for traditional academic accreditation, which is seen by many of us as a dead end street and a hindrance to being all that God wants us to be. Every June, educators representing about 40 schools and many apostolic networks come together to build relationships, share information and encourage each other.

♦ *Strategic Prayer Network (SPN).* Intercessors from all 50 states and numerous other countries are linked together in this network aimed at strategic intercession for world evangelization, currently for the 40/70 Window. International gatherings involving thousands have been held in Guatemala, Turkey and Germany, while others are planned for Bulgaria, Kazakhstan, Spain and Italy.

♦ *Apostolic Council of Prophetic Elders (ACPE).* An invitation-only group of up to 25 recognized prophets gather together each January to build relationships, share what they are hearing prophetically, and hold themselves accountable to one another for quality and integrity in their prophetic ministries.

♦ *Apostolic Roundtable of Deliverance Ministers (ARDM).* This affords an annual opportunity for a group of up to 25 invited deliverance ministers, who had previously operated quite independently from one another, to gather together every Fall, build relationships, and share mutual concerns.

♦ *International Coalition of Apostles (ICA).* Over 260 apostles, having passed through a strict nomination and invitation process, belong to ICA. I preside over an annual meeting held in Dallas the first week of December. Apostles gather to hear from each other, connect for ministry opportunities, and get their finger on the pulse of what the Spirit is saying to the churches.

♦ *New Apostolic Roundtable (NAR).* Since ICA is too large for a meaningful accountability group, smaller units are necessary to fulfill that purpose. I convene one of these, keeping the number of invited apostles to under 25, the week after Easter each year. Our

mutual accountability is based on personal relationships, and we look forward to seeing each other and
sharing what the Lord puts on our hearts.

♦ *Eagles' Vision Apostolic Team (EVAT).* As I was
organizing these six horizontal networks, it gradually
became clear that God was also asking me to give a
more vertical-type of apostolic covering to a small
number of apostles, but not to their churches or networks or ministries. EVAT, therefore, is somewhere
in between a horizontal and a vertical network—one
member suggested it might be "diagonal!" Unlike any
of the other six, EVAT members contribute financially
toward my salary.

It is important to mention, that (with the exception of
EVAT) my apostolic authority over the members of the groups
functions only in calling and presiding over the annual meet-
ings. When the meeting is over, I do not continue "covering"
the members any more than James continued to cover other
apostles such as Peter or Paul or John when they left the Council of Jerusalem.

2. Ambassadorial Apostles

Ambassadorial apostles have itinerant ministries which cata-
lyze and nurture apostolic movements on a broad scale. They
can do this on a national, regional, or international arena. John
Kelly of Ft. Worth, Texas serves with me in the leadership
team of ICA as an ambassadorial apostle. Suppose, for example, that a member of ICA in some part of the world wants
to call together the apostles of the region, possibly to establish

some kind of ongoing relational structure. To make this happen, it is often wise to call in an outsider who may be able, among other things, to neutralize whatever negative church politics might have arisen in that area. I am generally not available for this kind of ministry, but John Kelly is. He is often the catalyst necessary to spark an ongoing apostolic movement in different parts of the world.

Not only can an ambassadorial apostle help convene regional and international apostolic summits, but he or she is also available for trouble-shooting existing apostolic movements. Since one of the qualities of apostolic ministry is to "set things in order" as Paul told Titus to do (see Titus 1:5), ambassadorial apostles often receive divine revelation as to what action needs to be taken at a certain time and place. They frequently are able to turn a lose-lose situation into a win-win situation to the glory of God.

3. Mobilizing Apostles

Like ambassadorial apostles, mobilizing apostles are very willing to spend time on the road. They differ from ambassadorial apostles, however, in their focus on a specific cause or project. Chuck Pierce fulfills that function as the Mobilizing Apostle for the United States Strategic Prayer Network (USSPN). Working with me as the international SPN apostle and with Cindy Jacobs as the U.S. national apostle, Chuck frequently visits several states a month, meeting with state coordinators and intercessors. His goal is to mobilize 5,000 registered intercessors in each of the 50 states, linking them closely through electronic communication media, and he is well on his way toward reaching that goal.

4. Territorial Apostles

Some apostles have one of their primary apostolic spheres defined by a certain geographic territory. These territorial apostles have been given a great deal of authority within a city or a state or a nation or a region. Not only have they themselves accepted the responsibility that God has given them within that territory, but Christian leaders and even some secular leaders have also recognized and affirmed the extraordinary influence that they have in that particular society.

Two of the most outstanding territorial apostles with whom I am in contact are Bart Pierce of the city of Baltimore, Maryland and John Benefiel of the state of Oklahoma. Bart Pierce, for example, was publicly commissioned a bishop/apostle by a consortium of pastors representing the African-American churches of Baltimore. John Benefiel, in turn, was publicly awarded the honor of a Cheyenne name by the Southern Cheyenne in Oklahoma, the state which hosts the largest concentration of Native Americans in the nation.

Let me hasten to say that I don't believe God gives exclusive territorial jurisdiction to any one apostle. Bart Pierce is only one of several territorial apostles in Baltimore and John Benefiel likewise in the state of Oklahoma. Territorial apostles are so important that I will pick up on the role that they play in social transformation in the next chapter.

Hyphenated Apostles

I must not conclude this chapter without adding that many apostles have spiritual gifts, ministries, and activities assigned by God that cover more than one category.

First, many apostles have been given other gifts, and even offices, alongside their gift and office of apostle. I have the gift of teaching, for example, and I still see teaching as my primary ministry. I, therefore, see myself as a teacher-apostle. Bill Hamon is one of the nation's most recognized prophets, and he describes himself as a prophet-apostle. Michael Fletcher, the apostle over Grace Churches International out of Fayetteville, North Carolina, is also senior pastor of Manna Church. He is an apostle-pastor. Meanwhile, Ted Haggard still sees himself as a pastor-apostle.

Those who are recognized as apostles may also have more than one "ministry" or "activity" as I have defined them above. It is possible, for example, to be both a vertical and a horizontal apostle, although this is relatively rare. Mel Mullen of Red Deer, Canada, is an outstanding example. For years he was a vertical, ecclesiastical apostle over the Word of Life network of churches. More recently, however, he has also emerged as the apostle most anointed to bring together other apostles in Canada in a horizontal apostolic network.

Ted Haggard is an example of an apostle who functions in three of the eight apostolic "activities." He is a congregational apostle (New Life Church)-ecclesiastical apostle (Association of Life Giving Churches)-territorial apostle (city of Colorado Springs). Ché Ahn of Pasadena, California is a congregational apostle (Harvest Rock Church)-vertical apostle (Harvest International Ministries)-functional apostle (The Call). There are many others who have similar combinations of apostolic activities. They are "hyphen-ated apostles"

Apostles are far from being all the same. In God's kingdom today we have many apostles who exercise their ministry in many spheres.

Notes

[1] See *Churchquake!* by C. Peter Wagner (Ventura CA: Regal Books, 1999), pp. 141-143.

[2] Jim Laffoon, *A Divine Alliance* (Colorado Springs CO: Wagner Publications, 2001), p. 64.

[3] For details on breaking the 200 barrier, see Part 1 "Overcoming Small Church Barriers of 200 People by C. Peter Wagner," *The Everychurch Guide to Growth* by Elmer Towns, C. Peter Wagner & Thom Rainer (Nashville TN: Broadman & Holman Publishers, 1998), pp. 21-70.

[4] Lyle E. Schaller, *The Multiple Staff and the Larger Church* (Nashville TN: Abingdon Press, 1980), p. 28.

[5] Gary L. McIntosh, *One Size Doesn't Fit All* (Grand Rapids MI: Fleming H. Revell, 1999), p. 65.

CHAPTER EIGHT

APOSTLES FOR SOCIAL TRANSFORMATION

A s I mentioned in the last chapter, I believe that recognizing and affirming territorial apostles will be a major step in tuning in to what God wants to do in the decade of the 2000s. Right next to that will be recognizing and affirming marketplace apostles. Here I want to explain, as best I can, why this kind of apostolic leadership is necessary if our dreams for social transformation are going to come true.

Our Goal: Social Transformation

During the 1990s the idea that the kingdom of God is not confined to the four walls of the local church began to take hold strongly among Christian leaders. We began to take our prayer,

"Your kingdom come, Your will be done on earth as it is in heaven" more seriously than we had in the past. We believed that not only did God desire to save the lost and bring them into our churches, but that He also desired to change the world we live in for the better.

We began to talk about "city taking," and "city reaching," and "community transformation." But gradually, toward the end of the decade, "social transformation" seemed to be the most satisfactory way of expressing our outreach goal. The renowned *Transformations* video, produced by George Otis, Jr.'s Sentinel Group, helped sharpen our thinking. "Social transformation" includes all of the other terms, but it is broader. It encompasses spiritual transformation (both church growth and public morality), economic transformation, educational transformation, and governmental transformation. This can be applied to neighborhoods, cities, regions, and nations. The most manageable unit of them all is still probably the city, so I will focus on city transformation in this chapter.

Our Premise: Territorial Apostles

The major purpose of this book is to affirm that there are individuals today, just as there were in biblical times, who have been given the gift and office of apostle. This implies that, among other things, they have been entrusted with an extraordinary amount of spiritual authority in the body of Christ, but this authority only functions under divine anointing when it is exercised within the apostle's God-assigned sphere or spheres.

Knowing this highlights the importance of understanding apostolic spheres as much as possible, and I made an attempt to open some of the doors to this in the last chapter. One of the spheres in which some apostles serve the body of Christ is territorial, so it is proper to surmise that we have such a thing as "territorial apostles" among us.

Paul

We do have some rather straightforward biblical examples of territorial spheres. Paul, for instance, suggests to the Corinthians that he does not consider himself an apostle to the whole world or to the whole body of Christ. "We, however," he says, "will not boast ("boast" refers to boasting about apostolic authority as we see a few verses earlier [2 Cor. 10:8]) beyond measure, but within the limits of the sphere which God appointed us—a sphere which especially includes you" (2 Cor. 10:13). Corinth was a city in the Roman province of Achaia. Other provinces which we know were included in Paul's apostolic sphere of authority were Macedonia, Asia, and Galatia. Notice, as I have said before, that Paul's sphere would not include places like Alexandria or Jerusalem or Rome or any number of other cities or provinces where churches had by then been planted.

Titus

Titus, a member of Paul's apostolic team, operated as an apostle in the territory of Crete. Paul writes to him, "For this reason I left you in Crete, that you should set in order the things that are lacking, and appoint elders in every city as I commanded you (Titus 1:5). But Titus might have had other territorial spheres as well. His name is frequently mentioned in connection with Corinth. Paul had sent him there to trouble shoot, and then he writes back to them from Philippi, saying, "Nevertheless God, who comforts the downcast, comforted us by the coming of Titus" (2 Cor. 7:6). Paul's obvious relief suggests that Titus probably did some fruitful apostolic work in Corinth. There is also a strong hint in Paul's last epistle that another of Titus' territorial spheres could have been Dalmatia (modern Yugoslavia) (see 2 Tim. 4:9).

Peter

Likewise, Peter lists what are undoubtedly his own major territorial jurisdictions when he writes 1 Peter. He begins the letter: "Peter, an apostle of Jesus Christ, to the pilgrims of the Dispersion in Pontus, Galatia, Cappadocia, Asia, and Bithynia" (1 Pet. 1:1). It is interesting to observe that Peter doesn't mention Achaia or Macedonia, two of Paul's spheres.

Cultural Spheres

Just as interesting, however, is the fact that Peter *does* mention the other two of Paul's provinces, Galatia and Asia. This could lead us to deduce that within *territorial* spheres there can also be *cultural* spheres. Look at the words in Peter's greeting: "to the pilgrims of the Dispersion." This means that his epistle is directed specifically, not to the

Gentiles, but to the Diaspora Jews who were located in the five provinces he mentions. Paul, who was an apostle to the *uncircumcision*, was assigned to the *Gentiles* who lived in Galatia and Asia. Peter, who was an apostle to the *circumcision*, was assigned to the *Jews* who lived in the same provinces.

City Transformation

With this in mind, let's take a look at the state of affairs in regard to our efforts across America toward city transformation.

The widespread interest in city transformation began in 1990 with the publication of John Dawson's best seller, *Taking our Cities for God* (Creation House). During the decade of the 1990s virtually every major city in America launched

---

Territorial apostles are the ones who most likely will provide the persevering leadership that is required for city transformation.

---

a city transformation project of one kind or another. Some of the finest of the nation's Christian leadership was involved up front. A quality library emerged with authors such as Francis Frangipane and Ed Silvoso and George Otis, Jr. and Jack Dennison and Jack Hayford and Ted Haggard and Frank Damazio and many others joining in to help point the way. Mission America also launched a major nationwide project aimed at city transformation.

It looked to many of us as if the 1990s would see tangible answers to the prayer "Thy kingdom come" in city after city. But it didn't happen. In fact, after ten years of intense effort, it would be difficult to pinpoint cities or communities in America that have been transformed (past tense) as a result of proactive, strategic planning. One result of this is that we seem to be experiencing an epidemic of transformation fatigue. Some are throwing up their hands in despair.

Persevering Leadership

Our front line researcher for social transformation is George Otis, Jr., and a major vehicle for his reports are documentary videos. His first one, *Transformations,* has sparked powerful movements for changing society in many parts of the world. In that video he reports on four cities in various stages of transformation, with one of them, Almolonga, Guatemala, unquestionably deserving to be classified as "transformed" in the past tense, in the sense that it likely would be so described by a disinterested sociologist.

One of George Otis' extremely useful discoveries was a list of five commonalities of cities experiencing significant stages of transformation. They are persevering leadership; fervent, united prayer; social reconciliation; public power encounters, and diagnostic research (spiritual mapping). The first two were common to all the cities researched and the last three were common to 90 percent. I want to focus here on the first commonality, persevering leadership, in an attempt to show that territorial apostles are, at least in my mind, essential for successful, proactive city transformation.

Theological Compass Points

The accelerated and widespread efforts toward city transformation in the 1990s surfaced what I would consider three theological compass points which now mold our thinking about the way we develop strategies for our cities. Each one, however, carries an important "however."

- *Unity of the body of Christ is a prerequisite for social transformation.* However, we have also discovered that not any unity at all will do. We can end up with either functional unity or dysfunctional unity. I'll come back to that later.

- *The church of the city or region is spiritually one church with multiple congregations.* However, the idea of the city church can be unwisely applied, precipitating debilitating egalitarianism. More later.

- *The foundation of the church is apostles and prophets (Eph. 2:20).* However, this applies to city transformation in two dimensions: apostles of the *nuclear* church and apostles of the *extended* church or marketplace.

Apostles, Not Pastors, Are the Gatekeepers

City transformation will rise or fall on persevering leadership. This pivotal phrase, which I have italicized, combines verbiage from my two friends, John Maxwell and George Otis, Jr.

If this is true, a central question becomes: Who, then, are the God-appointed leaders or "spiritual gatekeepers" of the city?

I am afraid that we reached a misguided answer to this question in the 1990s. Our assumption then was that the local church pastors were the spiritual gatekeepers of the city. I even carried this questionable idea into my book *Apostles of the City* (Wagner Publications), which was released in 2000.

One reason why many agreed with this conclusion in the 1990s is that back then we were only beginning to learn about apostles. We knew there was a church of the city all right, but we were not mature enough to understand that the God-given foundation of that church is apostles and prophets (see Eph. 2:20). Nor was the governmental order clear to us: "*First* apostles, *second* prophets, *third* teachers..." (1 Cor. 12:28). We were actually getting it backward! Since most pastors who preach weekly sermons function also as teachers, they fit quite well into the third category. Biblically, 1 Corinthians 12:28 shows that the true spiritual gatekeepers of the city are apostles, not pastors (or teachers). Territorial apostles are the ones who most likely will provide the persevering leadership that is required for city transformation.

Weaknesses of the Pastoral Approach

Not only is it unbiblical to assume that pastors are the spiritual gatekeepers of the city, but this concept has not worked well in practice. Our disappointing experiences during the decade of the 1990s has turned up three practical weaknesses to the pastoral approach:

♦ *Misapplying the valid concept of the city church.* The problem came when once we discovered that the church of the city was one church with multiple congregations, we then made the mistake to assume that all local church pastors were, ipso facto, "co-pastors" of the city church. This meant that the losers had just as much to say about what to do and when as the winners. It succeeded in stonewalling the recognition of true leadership.

♦ *The Billy Graham committee model.* For over 40 years, the most effective model for accomplishing a true city-wide inter-church project was the Billy Graham committee. It worked for two reasons: it had strong leadership and it had a united vision. But both the top leadership and the vision were provided by an agency located *outside* of the city. The city pastors functioned basically, not as the leaders but as the supporting cast for the leader who would come to their city for a week or so. This worked well for one event, but it does not work for city transformation. For city transformation a switch is needed from outside leadership to inside leadership, from event-orientation to process-orientation, and from administrative and diplomatic leaders to risk-taking leaders.

♦ *The pastors' prayer summits.* In city after city the most appealing way to begin the process of city transformation seemed to be the pastors' prayer summit, originally designed by Joe Aldrich of Portland, Oregon. The premise was that if we only could get the pastors of the city praying together, God would then respond with city transformation. That hope never fully materialized for two reasons: (1) no one was allowed to come to present an agenda (such as city transformation) to the group, and (2) the focus was devotional and relational, but, by design, not task-oriented. The result was that we did see a great deal of united prayer, but without united vision.

Functional and Dysfunctional Unity

No one whom I know would disagree with the premise that unity of the body of Christ is a divine prerequisite for city transformation. But not all have agreed on the form that this unity should take.

I now see the difference between two forms of unity that I did not see in the 1990s:

♦ *Pastoral unity.* Pastoral unity is mercy-motivated, relational, politically correct, compromising, polite, and peaceful.

♦ *Apostolic unity.* Apostolic unity is task-oriented, visionary, aggressive, uncompromising, warlike, and often abrasive.

One of the major differences between the two is that in the paradigm of pastoral unity, unity can, and frequently does, become an end in itself. In the paradigm of apostolic unity, unity is only a means toward a higher end which is the task at hand. Apostles will recognize that the perceived need for pastors to build personal relationships across unfamiliar social, racial, denominational, cultural, and church-size lines is good, but it should not be regarded as a prerequisite for social transformation. Apostles also know that a workable process of reaching the whole city does not require one hundred percent of the churches, nor, in many cases even a majority of them

Apostolic Unity

While those who lean toward pastoral unity can find some supporting scriptures, apostles will focus on texts such as Jesus' prayer in John 17 where He prays, "that they all may be one, as You, Father are in Me, and I in You; that they also may be one in Us, that the world may believe that You sent Me" (Jn. 17:21). Unity is not the end, world evangelization is the end and whatever kind of unity ends up helping implement world evangelization is the kind that Jesus was praying for. Jesus actually said, "Do not think that I came to bring peace on earth. I did not come to bring peace but a sword" (Mt. 10:34).

This concept seems to play out fairly consistently in the history of the church. The major movements of God throughout history generally did not produce unity in the body of Christ, but rather they precipitated serious division. Take, for example, the Reformation with Martin Luther or the Methodists with John Wesley or the Presbyterians with John Knox or the Salvation Army with William Booth or the Azusa Street revival which initiated world-wide Pentecostalism. All of the above were apostolic-type movements.

The cities high on the scale of transformation, which George Otis has researched, rarely, if ever, began their process only after a successful effort at unifying the churches of their region. Those who became persevering leaders of their cities more often than not first provoked division, as apostolic leaders are prone to do.

Even though they did not begin this way, one of the outcomes of these movements of God was usually unity. However, it was not typically a pastoral-type of unity. The resulting unity was usually shaped into a new wineskin, much to the consternation of those remaining in the old wineskins.

Hidden Costs of Pastoral Unity

The pastoral mindset takes comfort in scriptures like "Behold, how good and how pleasant it is for brethren to dwell together in unity" (Ps. 133:1). They like to meet together, eat together, pray together, confess their sins to each other, exchange pulpits, and love each other. These relationships may seem so much like the fruit of the Spirit that they can gradually acquire an aurora of shekinah glory and when that happens, meeting together can become something that must be preserved, whatever the cost.

One of the hidden costs of preserving this kind of pastoral gathering is avoiding whatever could potentially be divisive. This inexorably requires the bonding of the group to be geared to the least common denominator. Consequently, we commonly see groups of pastors who are traditional, white, middle-class, Republican, denominational evangelicals. They would like to think that they represent the whole city, but most frequently they don't. Their leadership is typically consensus-building and maintenance-oriented. The chief duty of the leaders is to preserve the status quo in the most stimulating way possible!

Invisible Walls of Division

Ironically, such groups of city leaders in which, to use a George Otis phrase, "courtesy trumps conviction," can unwittingly produce division. Rarely do these groups attract the active participation of the most creative and influential Christian leaders of the city. Some show up at first, motivated perhaps by a guilty conscience and a feeling of obligation. But soon they gradually self-exclude from the group. They are not driven out—they draw themselves out. They are repeatedly invited back, but they claim that they do not have the time, despite the fact that members of hardly any other profession in the United States dispose of more personal discretionary time than do pastors. The deep down issue is not time; it is really priority.

Who, exactly, are those who have tended to exclude themselves from citywide pastoral gatherings? There are at least six kinds of leaders who quite frequently turn out to have higher priorities:

♦ *Vision-driven pastors.* Most of them quickly become restless with patching up old wineskins and preserving the status quo.

♦ *Task-oriented pastors and parachurch leaders.*
They clearly see that prioritizing unity at all costs will
not help them accomplish their task.

♦ *Influential minority leaders.* They perceive that presence without power is a form of tokenism. Almost
every city-wide gathering includes some minority leaders who have a special grace to build bridges to other
segments of society, but rarely are they the movers
and shakers within their own minority communities.

♦ *Pastors of dynamic, growing megachurches.* Their
personal agendas are usually in a different solar sys-
tem from 90% of American pastors. The communication gap is virtually impossible to surmount.

♦ *Charismatic pastors.* The group typically embraces
the distinctives of evangelical pastors, but requires that
charismatic pastors check their distinctives at the door
in order to preserve the least common denominator.
This makes the typical meeting more boring than some
can handle!

♦ *Apostles.* They find themselves outside of their apostolic spheres, and consequently they cannot function
as apostles within the pastorally-oriented group.

When these six kinds of leaders do not show up, even after
they are personally invited, the gossip starts. They frequently
may be characterized as "indifferent" or on "ego trips" or "em-
pire builders" or "tooting their own horn" or "they don't be-

lieve in the church of the city" or "if they don't lead it, they don't join it." That last statement is true, however, when you think of it. They are *leaders*! Asking them to join a group and not lead is like asking a singer to join the choir and not sing. One unfortunate result of this invisible wall of division is that the .300 hitters of the Christian leadership of the city are excluded from the starting lineup! Little wonder that among America's cities desirous of seeing the power of God manifested in social transformation we have seen few winners.

Can We Make a Switch?

Since our pastor-oriented approaches of the 1990s have not produced the expected results, can we switch to a new paradigm? Can we begin the process of recognizing that apostles are the foundation of the church in the city?

If we can, we will do well to bring two kinds of apostles into the equation, namely territorial apostles and marketplace apostles. Let me say up front that if we decide to make the switch we must realize that we are still in the beginning stages. In fact, the concept of marketplace apostles is so new that I do not feel able to say much more about them other than I feel sure they exist. There are some concepts about identifying territorial apostles, however, that I believe will be valuable for opening doors for recognizing and affirming them.

It is important to keep in mind that not all apostles *in* a city are also apostles *of* the city. Not all ecclesiastical apostles or functional apostles or mobilizing apostles or vertical apostles also have a *territorial* sphere. I am one case in point. I am an apostle who lives in Colorado Springs, Colorado, but God has not assigned my city to me as one of my apostolic spheres.

It is likewise important to recognize that every city, in all likelihood, will have several territorial apostles assigned to it, not just one. That means that different apostles *of* a given city will have different sub-spheres within the city. One apostle of the city, for example, may operate in the black community, another in the Hispanic community, and yet another in the white community, just as in the province of Asia Paul's sphere was Gentiles and Peter's sphere was Jews.

Other sub-divisions are likely, especially as the size of the city in question increases. One apostle might be recognized among evangelicals, for example, and another among charismatics. One's sphere might be in the northern part of the city and another's in the south. Another's might be the youth of the city. On and on. The point is that all of these territorial apostles have been assigned by God to their spheres, and it is understandable that God would be hesitant to answer prayers for the city if His design for spiritual authority there has not been honored.

Territorial Commitment

How can we recognize who are the bona fide territorial apostles of our city? It goes without saying that they must exhibit the qualities of every apostle that I have been describing in this book. Beyond that, however, territorial apostles must pass the test of territorial commitment.

Bob Beckett of Hemet, California (one of the cities featured on the *Transformations* video), has written the textbook on territorial commitment called *Commitment to Conquer* (Chosen Books). In it he makes a convincing argument that spiritual authority in a given region is proportional to the degree of territorial commitment of the Christian leader.

This applies first of all to local church pastors, who across the board, at least in America, exhibit a relatively low level of territorial commitment. What do I mean? As a starter, something like 90 percent of American pastors do not expect to be in their present parish ten years from now. Southern Baptists, our largest denomination, for example, show an average pastoral tenure of 2.7 years. United Methodist pastors (the second largest denomination) have a tenure of 3.4 years, and so on. Relatively few pastors have the lifetime commitment to their community that most dentists, lawyers, automobile dealers, law enforcement officers, or general contractors take for granted, just to name a few.

Secondly, territorial commitment applies even more strictly to territorial apostles than it would to local church pastors. In my mind it would be just as difficult to imagine a blind surgeon or a stuttering radio announcer or an obese beauty queen as it would be to imagine an apostle of the city not committed to the city.

Three Fishing Pools

In light of this, what should we do?

It is not up to us to create apostles. Only God does that by giving them the gift of apostle and by assigning them their apostolic spheres. But it is definitely up to us to recognize the apostles that God has given to the church, in this case to the church of the city, to encourage them, to award them the office when appropriate, and to submit gratefully to the authority of the apostle who is over whatever territorial sphere in which we might find ourselves as individuals. When we do this, the government will be in place to receive the powerful outpouring of the Holy Spirit on our cities.

As we begin to look for territorial apostles, let's look in the right places. I perceive that there are three major fishing pools in which we might be likely to find territorial apostles. Before I list them, let me say as clearly as I know how that these are not the *only* three places where territorial apostles will be found. Furthermore, not all genuine apostles in these three "fishing pools" will have been assigned by God to be apostles *of* the city. Many of them will have other apostolic spheres. These three, however are a good place to start:

- ♦ *Megachurch pastors.* Church growth research has shown that, across the board, the larger the church the longer the pastoral tenure. Check it out. Most pastors of churches of 1,000 or 2,000 or more have long since stopped looking for "greener pastures." They see their call to that congregation as a lifetime assignment. They have passed the test of territorial commitment. Furthermore those among them who pastor dynamically growing megachurches would also fit the definition of "congregational apostles" which I explained in the last chapter.

- ♦ *Parachurch leaders.* Not all parachurch leaders are apostles, but some are. Among them, some may have been assigned by God to the city in which they minister as their apostolic sphere. One of the better known at this point in time is Doug Stringer of Somebody

Cares in Houston, Texas. He has established a strong track record of territorial commitment and effective ministry toward social transformation in Houston.

♦ *Marketplace apostles.* It is helpful to recognize that the church of the city takes shape in both the nuclear church form (the local church) and the extended church form (believers in the marketplace). We are becoming tuned in quite well to apostles of the nuclear church, but we have some catching up to do in the extended church. I believe this will happen quite quickly, and when it does, our dreams of transformed cities all across the nation will begin to come true.

May God speed the day!

CHAPTER NINE

CONCLUSION: NEW WINE FOR NEW WINESKINS

The notion that there are apostles in today's church is not yet common currency. Only a very small fraction of practicing pastors were taught about apostles in their seminary or Bible school education. Yes, they learned about the apostles who lived in the first century or so, but they were also taught that the gift and office of apostle, as well as that of prophet, ceased at the end of the apostolic age.

This is changing, as I explained in some detail in the first chapter. In my way of thinking, we have now entered a New Apostolic Age, and the form that the church is now taking can be called the "New Apostolic Reformation." I use "Reformation" because we are now witnessing the most radical change in the way of doing church since the Protestant Reformation back in the 16th Century.

God Creates New Wineskins

Let's apply some biblical language to what we see taking place. We are fortunate enough to have a front row seat as we watch God creating, forming, and expanding a major new wineskin for the church. This is not a new thing for God. As we trace Christian history, it becomes evident that God has constantly been creating numerous new wineskins for His church over the 2000 years it has been spreading around the world. He is now doing it again.

The phrase "new wineskins" comes from Matthew 9 when the disciples of John the Baptist came to Jesus upset. One of the things that upset them was that they were so hungry. John the Baptist made them fast all the time. They complained to

---

God will only bless us if we let the wine go to our hearts and produce the fruit of the Holy Spirit. We must move forward in humility, honoring, while not necessarily imitating, those who have gone before.

Jesus that, while they were constantly fasting, Jesus' disciples were having a good time eating and drinking! What was going on?

Jesus first explained to them some things concerning the bride and the bridegroom, then he came to the part about wineskins. He said, "People [do not] put new wine into old wineskins, or else the wineskins break, the wine is spilled, and the wineskins are ruined. But they put new wine into new wineskins and both are preserved" (Mt. 9:17).

Here He was obviously referring to John the Baptist, the last prominent representative of the Old Covenant. John and his disciples represented what Jesus called an "old wineskin" while Jesus had come to introduce the New Covenant, a "new wineskin."

Old Wineskins Are Good.

It is important to keep in mind that Jesus was not drawing a line between good and bad. Jesus loved John the Baptist. In fact he once said, "Among those born of women, there has not risen one greater than John the Baptist" (Mt. 11:11). In other words, Jesus loved the old wineskin. The only thing about it was that it was not going to receive the new wine.

When we apply this to the New Apostolic Reformation, the new wineskin, it helps immensely to keep in mind that the old wineskins, which are the traditional denominations, are good. God loves them. They were at one point in time the new wineskins. When they were, they received God's new wine. But God is no longer pouring His new wine into them because of His mercy. He loves the old wineskins so much that he doesn't want to break them. He wants the traditional denominations to continue being a blessing to the body of Christ as long as they possibly can.

Some May Object

It should neither surprise nor offend those who agree with the kinds of things being revealed in books like this one and many others like it that some old wineskin Christian leaders may be prone to raise their voices in objection. After all, they have

given their lives to serving God in their traditional denominations or under their traditional mission boards, and they have
become comfortable with the way these structures operate for
the glory of God. No question that they have been ministering in God's will and that they should continue to do so. However, the thought of the gift and office of apostle actually
operating in the church today understandably pulls them out
of their comfort zone just as much as the lifestyle of Jesus'
disciples pulled John the Baptist's disciples out of their comfort zone. Jesus didn't despise them in the least for it.

Jesus also said that to whom much is given, much is required. A good deal of new wine is now being poured into the
modern apostolic movement. One of the things this requires
is that we assiduously avoid letting the wine go to our heads
and thereby come to imagine that we are in some way supe-
rior to those yet in old wineskins. No. God will only bless us
if we let the wine go to our hearts and produce the fruit of the
Holy Spirit. We must move forward in humility, honoring,
while not necessarily imitating, those who have gone before.
The kingdom of God has plenty of room for old wineskins,
new wineskins, and those in between.

Esteeming Each Other

If we do not falter in esteeming each other as Jesus esteemed
John the Baptist, God will be able to use all of His people,
regardless of their chosen wineskin, to maximize their personal and corporate effectiveness for the advance of His kingdom around the earth. All will be winners and the nations of
the world will be blessed!

SUBJECT INDEX